Debian 7: System Administration Best Practices

Learn the best ways to install and administer a Debian Linux distribution

Rich Pinkall Pollei

[PACKT] PUBLISHING
open source
community experience distilled

BIRMINGHAM - MUMBAI

Debian 7: System Administration Best Practices

First published: October 2013

Production Reference: 1181013

Published by Packt Publishing Ltd.
Livery Place
35 Livery Street
Birmingham B3 2PB, UK

ISBN 978-1-78328-311-8

`www.packtpub.com`

Cover Image by Vivek Sinha (`vs@viveksinha.com`)

Credits

Author
Rich Pinkall Pollei

Reviewers
Arturo Borrero González
Daniele Raffo
Ron Savage

Acquisition Editor
Rubal Kaur

Commissioning Editor
Govindan K

Technical Editors
Rohit Kumar Singh
Harshad Vairat

Project Coordinator
Romal Karani

Proofreader
Kevin McGowan

Indexer
Rekha Nair

Graphics
Sheetal Aute

Production Coordinator
Aditi Gajjar

Cover Work
Aditi Gajjar

About the Author

Rich Pinkall Pollei's over 40 year interest in computer hardware and software began in high school with Ohio Scientific's release of the first kit-built computers in the early 1970s. Later, he progressed to other systems, learning all he could of both the underlying hardware and software architectures, eventually working as a consulting programmer on some of the early time-sharing systems, first at the college he attended, and later when he worked as a Psychiatric Social Worker for the Tri-County Human Services Center in Reedsburg, Wisconsin.

Eventually, he decided to move into Information Technology as a permanent profession. He started as the Assistant Manager of Data Entry for Wisconsin Dairy Herd Improvement Cooperative at a time when such departments were common. He stayed with that company in various positions involving systems programming and analysis, and continued to learn. He was an official Beta Tester for Windows 3.0. Later, he set up the company's first Internet e-mail system using a discarded computer and modem, and the free version of Red Hat Linux. Total cost, not counting the dial-up account and his time, was $0, demonstrating that: "We who have done so much with so little for so long are now prepared to do absolutely anything with nothing".

Eventually, Wisconsin DHIA became AgSource Cooperative Services, which soon combined with other dairy industry-related cooperatives under a holding cooperative known as Cooperative Resources International (CRI). Rich continued to study and learn as computers and networking grew to greater importance in both our personal and business lives. For a number of years, he served as an official on the Unite Conference Planning committee (Unite is an independent, Unisys User Group).

Today, his official position is as a Security Analyst and Systems Engineer in the Infrastructure department of Information Technology for CRI, and he is approaching his 35th year with the company (or its predecessors). As such, he administers a number of Debian Linux servers, manages the official Internet infrastructure (he has one of the oldest individual handles still in use by an original registrant at ARIN), and consults on hardware issues, software internals, networking problems, and system and network security. He is a member of the Association for Computing Machinery (ACM), and has contributed code to several free software projects, including the Linux kernel, Blender, Vega Strike, and the Novell Core Protocol Filesystem utilities for Linux.

When not playing with computers, he is a science geek, plays chess, writes and arranges music, sings and plays saxophone and percussion in a local music group, collects old-fashioned books and board games, and is a licensed pilot.

This book would not have been possible without the support of my wife, Patricia, who gave up a good deal of our social time, since my day job required me to write it outside of normal working hours. Thanks, also, go to Sharvari Tawde of Packt Publishing, for encouraging me to take the plunge and write my first, full book, and the rest of the crew at Packt Publishing for helping me through the rough spots. I'd also like to thank my co-workers, especially Kathleen Anderson and Jean Banker, who provided encouragement when I was first offered the opportunity to write this book. Finally, to Louie and Tinkerbelle, the family cats who forced me to take periodic breaks by jumping on the computer keyboard and demanding attention.

About the Reviewers

Arturo Borrero González has been working in the IT environment for almost 5 years now, always with Linux systems.

He is interested in networking and high availability clusters.

For the last 3 years, Arturo's job has been in Centro Informático Científico de Andalucía (CICA), the regional National Research and Education Network (NREN) of Andalusia (Spain). There, he does system administration for the Network Information Security department.

He loves Debian and free/open-source software.

Currently he is collaborating with the Netfilter project. Also, he's trying to get his degree in IT engineering at the University of Seville.

Daniele Raffo has been a happy Linux user since the mid-1990s, and now an LPIC certified Linux Professional. Holder of a Ph.D. in Computer Science and former CERN civil servant, he also has experience in the fields of networking, security, and Java programming. He is the lead author of the official Handbook for Enigmail, the OpenPGP plugin for Mozilla applications.

I would like to thank my parents and Renata for their support, and Linus Torvalds for his extraordinary idea.

Ron Savage is a semi-retired programmer who has been writing software in Perl for a number of decades.

He has a degree in mathematics (astrophysics), but has always worked as a programmer.

He has found that, even using Perl, he still has to write a lot of Bash, SQL, JavaScript, HTML, and CSS to design and build databases for servers such as Postgres.

Nevertheless, while writing Perl he's had great fulfillment, and endless opportunities for expressing creativity, and has enjoyed almost every single day's work. Yes, even the hard days.

He's always worked as a self-employed contractor, and has encountered a fascinating range of work. Some instances are:

At BHP (an Australian mining corporation), they bought some American 'Star Wars' technology which fired radar straight down from a plane into the sea, searching for Russian submarines. BHP adapted it to search for seams of minerals (on land), aimed down from a wooden glider towed by a (metallic) plane, and that required processing vast amounts of data, and new ways to visualize such data.

At Telstra (the dominant Australia-wide communications company) he wrote a lot of code to help maintain about 15,000 network routers scattered across the country, and which carry almost all Australian phone and Internet sessions.

Another contract was a pair of search engines written for Monash University, based in Melbourne. One is used by staff and students, and the other is dedicated to the telephonists. The latter uses the same database as the former, but also communicates with a number of PABXes.

Currently, he's working with Peter Stuifzand (in the Netherlands) on a short book called *The Marpa Guide*. Marpa is a recent, and astonishing, generic lexer and parser written by Jeffrey Kegler.

He also writes fiction and autobiographical works.

I'm indebted to my parents for providing a liberal-minded environment to grow up in, completely free from doctrinaire-style influences.

I'm also delighted to thank everyone who contributes to Open Source projects, in all their variety. It's a wonderful, global, and communal type of volunteering, and has provided me with a fascinating and fulfilling career.

One drawback of programming, though, is that it deals with concepts and activities incomprehensible to people of my parents' generation, and even to my friends, but the creativity makes up for that.

---

www.PacktPub.com

Support files, eBooks, discount offers and more

You might want to visit www.PacktPub.com for support files and downloads related to your book.

Did you know that Packt offers eBook versions of every book published, with PDF and ePub files available? You can upgrade to the eBook version at www.PacktPub.com and as a print book customer, you are entitled to a discount on the eBook copy. Get in touch with us at service@packtpub.com for more details.

At www.PacktPub.com, you can also read a collection of free technical articles, sign up for a range of free newsletters and receive exclusive discounts and offers on Packt books and eBooks.

PACKTLIB®

http://PacktLib.PacktPub.com

Do you need instant solutions to your IT questions? PacktLib is Packt's online digital book library. Here, you can access, read and search across Packt's entire library of books.

Why Subscribe?

- Fully searchable across every book published by Packt
- Copy and paste, print and bookmark content
- On demand and accessible via web browser

Free Access for Packt account holders

If you have an account with Packt at www.PacktPub.com, you can use this to access PacktLib today and view nine entirely free books. Simply use your login credentials for immediate access.

Table of Contents

Preface

The Debian Linux distribution is the most stable distribution available, and it is used on more Internet web servers than any other operating system. While there are many instructional web pages and cookbooks written about Linux, and Debian Linux in particular, it is too easy for new users and seasoned administrators to get lost in the details. This book provides a broad overview, more of a what to than a how to, of Debian Linux administration. The chapters are designed to cover the subjects an administrator must address, and include background information, tips and suggestions, and basic knowledge and administration techniques. References are included that cover the various topics in greater detail than can be included in a book of this length.

Although oriented towards the current Debian stable distribution, the subjects covered are useful for any Linux administrator to know. As for the lack of numerous, detailed examples, I apologize. It is impossible in a book of this length to go as far into details as I would have liked. Fortunately, the Debian Project provides excellent guides and references, as well as online web pages that are pointed out in the text.

What this book covers

Chapter 1, Debian Basics for Administrators, covers what distinguishes Debian from other Linux distributions, and delves into the background of the Debian Project and free software in general.

Chapter 2, Filesystem Layout, covers the two primary methods used to boot Intel 32- and 64-bit systems, the various Linux filesystem formats, disk partitioning, and data protection using disk, partition, and directory-based encryption.

Chapter 3, Package Management, covers the basics of Debian package management, including the management utilities and updating your system.

Chapter 4, Basic Package Configuration, covers common software configuration techniques, including the location of files and documentations, and trends in Debian configuration.

Chapter 5, System Management, covers important system management topics, including startup and shutdown, networking, filesystem maintenance, and display managers.

Chapter 6, Basic System Security, covers security issues important for system safety, including special packages available to assist in installing additional security software, firewall tools, and intrusion detection.

Chapter 7, Advanced System Management, briefly covers advanced management topics including remote backups, distributed configuration management, and clustering. It also includes coverage of Webmin, a web-based administration tool that is compatible with nearly all Linux installations.

What you need for this book

Although software is not required, this book covers the Debian 7 Linux distribution. All software referred to in this book, with the exception of Webmin, is available in the Debian stable release, available for download from the Debian Project web site (`http://www.debian.org/`). It is also available on CD, DVD, and Blu-ray Discs from vendors mentioned on that site. Webmin software is available from its own site (`http://www.webmin.com/`).

Access to the Internet is required if you are going to download the software, or if you wish to follow up with the various reference material and other documents mentioned in the book. In particular, beginners are encouraged to become familiar with the Debian installation guide (`http://www.debian.org/releases/stable/installmanual`) and the reference manual (`http://www.debian.org/doc/manuals/debian-reference/`), which are also available as documentation packages in the Debian distribution.

Who this book is for

This book is for users and administrators who are new to Debian, or for seasoned administrators who are switching to Debian from another Linux distribution. A basic knowledge of Linux or Unix systems is assumed. Since the book is a high-level guide, more of a what to than a how to, the reader should be willing to go to the referenced material for further details and practical examples.

Conventions

In this book, you will find a number of styles of text that distinguish between different kinds of information. Here are some examples of these styles, and an explanation of their meaning.

Code words in text are shown as follows: "Usually, this is added to a separate `webmin.list` file in `/etc/apt/sources.list.d`."

Any command-line input or output is written as follows:

```
# deb cdrom:[Debian GNU/Linux 7.0.0 "Wheezy" - Official amd64 \
  NETINST Binary-1 20130504-14:43]/ stable main
```

New terms and **important words** are shown in bold. Words that you see on the screen, in menus or dialog boxes for example, appear in the text like this: "Often, this is as simple as providing a standard configuration, such as Apache's simple **It works!** page."

[Warnings or important notes appear in a box like this.]

[Tips and tricks appear like this.]

Reader feedback

Feedback from our readers is always welcome. Let us know what you think about this book—what you liked or may have disliked. Reader feedback is important for us to develop titles that you really get the most out of.

To send us general feedback, simply send an e-mail to `feedback@packtpub.com`, and mention the book title via the subject of your message.

If there is a topic that you have expertise in and you are interested in either writing or contributing to a book, see our author guide on `www.packtpub.com/authors`.

Customer support

Now that you are the proud owner of a Packt book, we have a number of things to help you to get the most from your purchase.

Errata

Although we have taken every care to ensure the accuracy of our content, mistakes do happen. If you find a mistake in one of our books—maybe a mistake in the text or the code—we would be grateful if you would report this to us. By doing so, you can save other readers from frustration and help us improve subsequent versions of this book. If you find any errata, please report them by visiting `http://www.packtpub.com/submit-errata`, selecting your book, clicking on the **errata submission form** link, and entering the details of your errata. Once your errata are verified, your submission will be accepted and the errata will be uploaded on our website, or added to any list of existing errata, under the Errata section of that title. Any existing errata can be viewed by selecting your title from `http://www.packtpub.com/support`.

Piracy

Piracy of copyright material on the Internet is an ongoing problem across all media. At Packt, we take the protection of our copyright and licenses very seriously. If you come across any illegal copies of our works, in any form, on the Internet, please provide us with the location address or website name immediately so that we can pursue a remedy.

Please contact us at `copyright@packtpub.com` with a link to the suspected pirated material.

We appreciate your help in protecting our authors, and our ability to bring you valuable content.

Questions

You can contact us at `questions@packtpub.com` if you are having a problem with any aspect of the book, and we will do our best to address it.

1

Debian Basics for Administrators

"What is the best distribution for my needs? What do I need to know to administer a Debian system? What's different about Debian? What is the best way to handle something specific in Debian? I ran an Internet search on these questions and got millions of results. Now what do I do? Can someone help me?"

The answer to the last question is yes. Answering the others requires a bit of background. This discussion is oriented towards those who are new to Debian. In it, we'll cover Debian's place among the various Linux distributions, project organization (and how that impacts administration), and licensing issues. Those who are already familiar with Debian may wish to skip ahead to the next chapter.

Linux distributions

Debian is just one of many Linux distributions. Selecting which distribution is best for your deployment can be a rather daunting task. The reason for so many distributions is that the developers or sponsors of each have a different vision of which software should be installed by default, which software is appropriate for particular tasks, and how the system is best administered. This means that selecting a distribution that matches your purpose and preferences will make installation and administration easier.

> Any distribution can be made to reflect an administrator's preferences by installing non-default software or, in some cases, software not native to the distribution software and using non-default configurations. However, selecting an appropriate distribution means less effort is necessary to fulfill the administrator's requirements.

The three branches

Linux distributions can be broken down into three branches, named from their original distribution or their package managers: SLS, RPM, and DPKG.

SLS

The **Softlanding Linux System** (**SLS**) distribution, which evolved into the Slackware distribution, is one of the oldest. Distributions in this branch generally made minimal or no changes to the original software packages before including them. Distributions using this format generally provided no native software management and depended on third-party utilities for package management and administration. These utilities were readily available and often included, so this was not necessarily a disadvantage.

> These distributions are also known as Sorcerer/Lunar-Linux/Source Mage (SLS) distributions for the most common distributions using the format.

These distributions are mostly obsolete and not often seen. However, the package format is still used by many software projects.

RPM

The **Red Hat Package Manager** (**RPM**) was developed by Red Hat in order to provide some structure for software management. It provides all of the customary software management features which are as follows:

- Software installation, including resolution of software dependencies during the process
- Various reports on the installed software
- Software verification and control
- The ability for users to package their own software so that it can also be managed

Most RPM-based distributions are sponsored by a company that also sells an enhanced version of the distribution and provide extensive, paid support. This also means that unified administrative utilities are available, at least in the paid version, and often in the free version with somewhat reduced features. Many administrators prefer this approach, which makes most common administrative tasks available through a single starting place.

The most common distributions using this format are Red Hat (and the paid version, **Red Hat Enterprise Linux** or **RHEL**) and SuSE (the free version is known as OpenSuSE and the paid version is often referred to as **SuSE Linux Enterprise Server** or **SLES**).

DPKG or DEB

The **Debian Packaging System** (**DPKG/DEB**) was developed about the same time as the RPM, and has the same features, although they are implemented differently. DPKG refers to the original software packaging utility. This has been superseded by more flexible and user-friendly utilities, so this branch is often referred to by the extension used by the package files: DEB (`.deb`). Some distributions in this branch have corporate sponsorship (Ubuntu is the most notable) and thus, have a unified administrative utility, similar to SuSE's YaST for example. Others, such as Debian, depend upon third-party software to fulfill this function.

The most common distributions in this branch are Debian and Ubuntu. Most of the others in the branch, such as Mint and BackTrack, are derived from one of these.

Other differences

There are a couple of other things administrators should know about how Debian differs from other distributions before we get into details.

One thing to note is that the home of a distribution, if you will, can affect the character of a distribution. For example, Red Hat was originally developed in the United States and, as such, reflects the common usage and preferences of American administrators. SuSE, on the other hand, originated in Germany, and reflects European practices. A concrete example of this is that, for Red Hat, GNOME is the preferred window manager, while SuSE is more geared towards the KDE desktop manager, although both window managers, as well as others, are available in both distributions. The primary issue is that a distribution that matches your preferences will require fewer configuration changes or software package installations to match your administrative style. Information on a distribution's history and intended purpose can be found on the distribution's home page, and frequently in Wikipedia entries as well.

The Debian project originated in the United States, but recruited developers worldwide right from the beginning. Thus, defaults and settings reflect the most common best practices worldwide as much as possible, with individual packages reflecting the interpretation of their developer's particular experience.

The best practice is to select a distribution that best matches your preferences. That way, the default configuration will be closest to what you want, and will require less tweaking to match your administrative style.

Next, distributions fall into two main categories: those with corporate sponsorship, and those without it. Corporate sponsorship usually implies that paid support is available, as well as a paid version of the distribution with extra features. This does not mean that it is not available for distributions without such sponsorship, only that one must find third-parties that provide it rather than finding it in one place.

Debian does not have or accept corporate sponsorship, although it does accept and receive a great deal of corporate support in the form of hardware, developer support, and donations. The idea is that Debian is guided by their social contract and their developers, rather than a particular corporate sponsor. Paid support is available from a number of sources (many who have also contributed), and free support from the developers and user community is available via many support pages and forums, as well as an official bug reporting and tracking site.

Another thing that the lack of corporate sponsorship might imply is a lack of structure or direction. This is not the case for Debian. In fact, there is a very strong structure, with supporting processes and administrative responsibilities, guiding Debian development and release. The main impact is more subtle—Debian is guided by a social contract, and a community of developers committed to the idea of quality, free software, widely available, that runs as trouble-free as possible in as many environments as possible.

With that, let's take a look at the Debian Project itself.

The Debian Project

Debian is, at its heart, a totally free, volunteer-supported distribution. Unlike Ubuntu, Red Hat, or SuSE, it is not sponsored by any corporation. This does not mean it is any less organized. The Debian project is, in fact, well-organized, with a well-defined government, detailed standards and guidelines, and specified procedures for software release, maintenance, and support.

> The name *Debian* comes from the names of the project founder, Ian Murdock, and his wife Debra.

The social contract

Above everything else, Debian developers believe in free software, as defined by the Free Software Foundation. In essence, this definition ensures that users have the freedom to:

- Run the program for any purpose
- Study how the program works and make modifications
- Redistribute copies
- Distribute copies of modified versions

All of this is embodied in the Debian Social Contract, and the **Debian Free Software Guidelines** (**DFSG**), both of which may be found at `http://www.debian.org/social_contract`. All Debian developers commit to this social contract, which states the guiding principles for the Debian Project, and influences all decisions as to what's included in the distribution and how it is distributed and maintained. Of particular note are the provisions for non-free software, and support in many different computing environments.

The non-free provision not only allows for such software to run on Debian systems, but provides for special Debian repositories for that software which can be released without payment. Such software is, in fact, supported by Debian developers who package and support it. The primary distinction is that it is not a part of the official Debian distribution, due to licensing restrictions. Of course, software that must be paid for can also be run on Debian distributions. It just can't be included in the Debian repositories.

Constitution

The means of achieving the goals of the Debian Social Contract is outlined in the Debian Constitution. It lays out the formal structure and decision-making process. The project has a full organizational structure that includes Officers, Distribution, Publicity, Support, and Infrastructure divisions, with specific positions and responsibilities. Although Debian is an all-volunteer organization, it is every bit as organized as any large corporate entity.

Policies

In addition to the organization, there are very comprehensive policy manuals that guide everything about development and release, including the structure of the repositories and archives, as well as a number of related standards documents. Information on all of this is available at `http://www.debian.org/devel/`.

One of the most important effects of these policies, and the organization behind them, is the stability of the Debian distribution. At any one time, there are three main versions of Debian available: stable, testing, and unstable. There are also experimental and backports versions, but they are not complete distributions.

> The experimental version contains packages that are incomplete and not ready to be included in the unstable release. Backports contain newer packages compiled especially for the current Debian stable release.

The unstable version is where active development takes place. Once a package has no "release critical" bugs and works on all supported architectures, it is moved to testing, where it gets additional testing. At some point, the testing contents are frozen in preparation for a new stable release. After stability is verified and all packages satisfy Debian requirements for release, testing becomes the new stable release, and the cycle continues.

Requirements for the stable release are quite stringent. In fact, requirements for testing are strict enough as some have commented that the testing version is more stable than many companies' stable releases. Thus, in Debian, stable means just that. A stable release of Debian is extremely dependable, with a system for releasing security and emergency updates that keeps it so. It provides mission-critical, production quality software for servers and development systems. This is one of the main reasons Debian is used on more production web servers than any other Linux distribution (according to W3Tech, as of January 2012).

As with any advantage, there is a corresponding disadvantage. Debian stable does not always contain the latest, leading-edge software. This is done to ensure the distribution is as mature and crash-free as possible. Of course, it is possible to install newer software under Debian with its required dependencies. In fact, the backports set of repositories contains just such software, pre-compiled especially for use on the Debian stable release. Such packages, however, are not guaranteed to be as stable as those that comprise the official stable release.

Licensing

As mentioned in *The social contract* section, licensing is one of the central issues in Debian. All of the software in the official Debian distribution is released under any one of several free software licenses, usually some version of the GNU **General Public License** (**GPL**), a Berkeley BSD-style license, or some form of the artistic license used by some Perl developers.

What this means for administrators is that they can run Debian on as many different systems as they wish, without licensing fees, and provide as many copies as they wish to others, without restrictions (well, technically, there are restrictions, but mostly they are requirements that will keep the software free, in the spirit of the Free Software Foundation's definition).

This freedom does not prevent an administrator from running proprietary software in Debian. In fact, such freedom is a part of the social contract. The only restrictions are whatever that software's license states.

What happened to Firefox?

One of the best examples of how careful Debian is about licensing issues involves the Mozilla suite of software, which includes the Thunderbird mail reader and the popular Firefox browser. A whole chapter could be written on the history of the dispute and the issues involved. However, the basic problem is that the Mozilla artwork is not under a free license as defined by the Debian guidelines. For a while, Debian was allowed to use other artwork, but eventually the Mozilla Corporation withdrew that permission. Some of the reasons this changed included the way the Debian developers compiled the software to comply with their policies and the social contract.

After a long argument, the Debian project determined that the best approach was to rename the software, as allowed by the Mozilla license, so it would remain compatible with the DFSG. Thunderbird in Debian is now called Iceowl, and Firefox is called Iceweasel.

> The names evolved from early discussions when Iceweasel was used to describe a hypothetical re-branded version. The name stuck. Other Mozilla software was renamed in a similar fashion.

The advantages for administrators include the following:

- The Debian version is unencumbered by non-free licensing.
- Bugs are frequently fixed by the Debian maintainers more quickly. These patches are passed on to the Mozilla maintainers. This is actually required for all patches to any software by Debian developers by policy.
- Updates are managed via the Debian packaging framework rather than requiring a separate, proprietary update procedure.
- The software uses standard Debian system libraries rather than installing Mozilla's separate libraries.
- The software will run on the various Debian supported, non-Intel architectures. For example, do you have an old IBM z Series server? Debian Iceweasel will run on it. How about an old SG or Sparc workstation? Same story, Debian Iceweasel will run just fine.

Nevertheless, Debian Iceweasel is, for all practical purposes, Firefox. It offers the same look and feel, uses the same plugins, and identifies itself to servers as compatible with Firefox. The same is true for the rest of the re-branded Mozilla software.

> The Plugin Search feature is modified in Debian to seek only free plugins, but I've never found this to be a problem. Non-free plugins can still be installed at the user's own discretion, and will work.

Repositories

Another result of Debian's licensing policies is the existence of three distinct software repositories:

- **main**: These are packages whose license conforms to the DFSG
- **contrib**: These packages have licenses that also conform to the DFSG, but that depend on other packages or libraries that do not
- **non-free**: These are packages whose license does not conform to the DFSG but that are allowed to be distributed with Debian

Users are free to choose whether to allow software from the contrib and non-free classes to be installed. If it is installed, the users are responsible for knowing and following the appropriate licenses.

Other, non-official repositories also exist, which host software that, for one reason or another, isn't included in any of the official Debian repositories.

Debian environments

Debian includes as wide a variety of software as possible. As of this writing, the Debian stable distribution contains over 48,000 pre-compiled packages in the latest stable version. According to some counts, this is more than any other Linux distribution. To be fair, many of these are niche applications that do not have a wide user base. But the number of packages is only a part of the story.

The support of many different environments is also a distinguishing characteristic of Debian distributions, and probably one of the most startling. In fact, Debian is unique in the number of different processors supported. At the time of writing, they include both 32-bit and 64-bit Intel and AMD chips, ARM (EABI or little endian version), Intel Itanium, MIPS (both big and little endian), PowerPC (yes, this means it will run on IBM servers!), System/390 (the old IBM architecture), and SPARC. In addition, the Alpha architecture was supported up until Debian 6.0, and there are unofficial ports to other ARM architectures as well as Amtel's RISC chip (AVR32), HP's PA-RISC chip (up until Debian 6.0), the Motorola 68000, IBM system Z, and Hitachi SuperH processors. There is also support for FreeBSD as the primary operating system instead of Linux on Intel 32-bit and 64-bit architectures, and there are other unofficial or experimental non-Linux-based Debian distributions for the GNU Hurd operating system.

This commitment results in a distribution that is extremely flexible, which can be used in a great many environments. Because of this, the Debian developers have chosen not to design a default installation package suitable for most users. A default Debian install (with no optional software selected) includes only the basics. The administrator is expected to select as options, or install later, the appropriate software. This is not difficult as the base system includes everything necessary to easily install additional software.

This contrasts with Ubuntu Linux, which is based on Debian. A basic Ubuntu installation is designed to work out of the box for the majority of users. Thus, it includes more software, making it an appropriate distribution for a new Linux user without extensive knowledge of what may be available, or a preference for exploring what is there, as opposed to wading through packages offered for optional installation. However, this may also result in an installation with unnecessary components. Of course, they may be easily removed, but it is another example of choosing the proper distribution to reduce the administrator's workload.

This is one reason Debian is one of the major players in commercial servers, as only the software and services necessary are installed, which generally leads to better performance and simpler system management. This also means that Debian will run acceptably on older, poorer performing equipment. Note that, in spite of this, it is also most certainly possible to install a wide variety of software, both during and after installation, which will allow a Debian system to fulfill even the most insatiable developers.

Impact on administration

Now that we have the background on how Debian is organized and developed, the question to be answered is, "how does this affect the administrator."

There are three primary areas which an administrator needs to be aware of. They are as follows:

- The availability of support
- The availability of proprietary features
- Licensing issues

Debian support

The Debian Project has a very large and well-defined support structure that includes a lot of documentation, a Wiki, mailing lists and newsgroups, websites, and forums. Live help is available on IRC, and there is a well-developed and effective bug tracking system, usable by anyone. It is also possible to contact Debian developers and package maintainers directly, something not always possible with other distributions. These and other available support resources may be found at `http://www.debian.org/support`.

The thing to remember is that these are volunteers (some of them are, in fact, paid by companies that officially donate their time to the Debian Project). A major release occurs about every two years, and is supported with updates for three years, or about a year after the following major release. The response to bug reports and support requests, in my experience, is quite good, and sometimes faster than paid support. Of course, the quality of advice in places like the forums varies with the experience of the person giving the advice. Nevertheless, this works very well for the majority of users. The fact that Debian releases are extremely stable to begin with helps.

For those who prefer to pay for support, there are a number of companies and individuals that provide such a service. In fact, the Debian website has a page that lists such consultants all over the world.

In a similar vein, although Debian is freely available by downloading from any of the numerous Debian servers and mirror sites, and burning one's own set of installation CDs, DVDs, or Blue-ray discs from the images so obtained, it is also possible to purchase ready-made installation media from third-party vendors.

Proprietary features

Simply put, there is no paid version of Debian with extra features.

One of the side effects of this is that there is no official Debian-unified administration utility. SuSE, for example, provides YaST, and Ubuntu provides UCC. However, there are many configuration and administration tools available in the distribution, and the various window managers, such as GNOME and KDE gather their administrative menu entries in one place for easy use. Likewise, there are third-party applications that work well on Debian that bring most, if not all, common tasks into a single place with a unified and user-friendly interface.

Probably the most important issue the administrator will run into is the problem of supported hardware. While Debian attempts to support as wide a variety of hardware as possible, some manufacturers don't provide information on their proprietary hardware. Without such information (required to write a driver), if a manufacturer doesn't provide a Linux driver, it won't be supported in Debian.

> There are special cases. Certain Windows XP drivers can be used by Linux if they are available, but they require additional steps to install and activate them.

Actually, this isn't so much a Debian issue as a Linux issue. Some distributions that offer a paid version may include proprietary drivers in the enhanced version. However, in general, if your hardware is supported by Linux, it will work with Debian. There are a number of pages available on the Debian Wiki as well as other sites explaining how to get Linux and Debian to run on many systems with unusual hardware. Furthermore, with the gain in popularity of Linux, many manufacturers are providing the necessary drivers, if not free and with a license that allows them to be included in the base distribution, at least in a format that can be installed and used with Debian.

> Best practice: check hardware support lists and compatibility sites for Linux before purchasing hardware or installing any distribution.

Where to find installation help and information

So, how do you find out about supported hardware or what to do in case your hardware isn't supported during Debian installation? Probably the best starting place is the current Debian installation guide. Versions for all supported architectures in different languages are available at `http://www.debian.org/releases/stable/installmanual`, and they are quite thorough. Section 2.1 covers supported hardware, and includes links to more general Linux hardware compatibility sites. The chapter also links to section 6.4 in the same manual, which covers how to provide missing firmware during installation. Some of the architecture specific manuals mention the Linux Hardware Compatibility HOWTO, but some do not. It may be found at `http://www.tldp.org/HOWTO/Hardware-HOWTO/`. Finally, you may find additional information specific to each supported architecture for the current Debian release at `http://www.debian.org/releases/stable/releasenotes`.

Summary

Debian is an extremely stable Linux distribution that includes a great variety of software that runs in many different environments and on many different CPU architectures. It is free, in the spirit of the Free Software Foundation's definition, and thus may be run freely on as many systems as an administrator desires, without limit or licensing fees. It may be freely copied, modified, and re-distributed. Debian is available from many official Debian servers and mirrors, and it is well supported by an official and well-defined, albeit all-volunteer organization, which provides support via many channels. Paid installation media and support are also available from many third parties.

Debian installations tend to install the minimum services necessary, requiring the administrator to add any additional services necessary after the initial installation. This results in systems that are secure, run faster without unnecessary services, and allows Debian to work satisfactorily on older, less capable systems.

Now that we've covered the basics of Debian, it's time to cover the basics of disk layouts, including the structures used for booting and how to determine the partition layouts.

2
Filesystem Layout

Some of the first decisions that must be made, even before installing Debian, involve deciding the best way to format the storage space for the installation. This includes what type of filesystem to use, how to partition it for the best effect, and whether and what to encrypt for security. The actual work of partitioning and boot code placement is handled by the Debian installer, and can be altered later using standard Linux bootloader and partitioning utilities. The installation process and the utilities are covered well by the Debian installation guide mentioned in the previous chapter, and the documentations for the GRUB2, fdisk, and GNU Parted included with the appropriate software packages.

This chapter serves as a basic introduction to the concepts of boot loading and disk partitioning, along with some guidelines to keep in mind when installing Debian or updating your boot or partitioning schemes. Do not worry if you are still uncertain what is best for your situation when first installing Debian. As we shall see, the defaults will work just fine for most cases, and the beginner can't really go wrong while using them when in doubt.

Partition tables

Each architecture has its own characteristic method of partitioning disk drives and placing boot code in the appropriate place. For most, this is very straightforward. However, the Intel architecture is undergoing changes that require some understanding of the boot process and disk layout.

Single or multiboot

One of the first choices to be made when installing any Linux distribution is whether the system will be single or multiboot. In general, many developers run both Windows and Linux on the same machine. In some cases, due to licensing restrictions or just personal preference, they wish to use the Windows installation that came with their computer and boot into one or the other as needed. This is perfectly fine, and most bootloaders will recognize both operating systems and provide menu items to boot the desired one. Another option is to use Xen or similar virtualization software to boot both simultaneously. A third choice is to run Windows under a Linux **virtual machine** (**VM**) using QEMU or KVM software. Creating VMs under QEMU, KVM, Xen, or any other virtualization software (such as VMware), would be a complete book in itself. For our purpose, we will consider a VM as essentially equivalent to an actual hardware system, since the issues outside VM creation are identical.

> Best practice, if this is a single operating system server environment, will be a single-boot system. If this is a developer system that may require booting into an alternative operating system, use dual boot. VM generally does not require dual boot.

BIOS versus UEFI

Up until the late 1990s, the **Basic Input/Output System**, or **BIOS**, was the way all Intel-based systems were booted. Its disk partitioning information was held in a **Master Boot Record** (**MBR**) with additional code in the first sector of each bootable partition. With the advent of the Microsoft-sponsored Secure Boot feature, and its associated boot mechanism known as the **Universal Extensible Firmware Interface** (**UEFI**), there is a new partitioning layout, and additional considerations.

Boot code under BIOS

BIOS is the traditional boot method, and is well-supported by Debian. There are several choices for the placement of the boot code. Common practice is for it to be placed in the MBR at the beginning of the boot disk. However, if there are multiple operating systems already installed (especially Microsoft Windows), this replaces the installed bootloader with the one common to Linux. This is generally not a problem, since the installation and update process searches for other operating systems and includes the ability to boot them as an alternative in the boot menu.

> The current bootloader for Debian on Intel is called GRUB2, although other, older loaders exist and may be installed as an alternative.

However, there are occasions where the original, non-Linux bootloader is preferred. For example, some Windows installations won't update properly if a non-Windows bootloader is installed. In this case, the Linux boot code can be placed at the beginning of the Linux boot partition rather than the MBR at the beginning of the drive, where the non-Linux bootloader can usually find it and offer it as an alternative on its boot menu.

The problem of Windows updates when using the Linux GRUB2 bootloader is quite complex. The issue seems to occur primarily with major Internet Explorer version upgrades, and the reasons remain unclear, at least in any discussions and bug reports I've been able to find. Adding to the problem is the occasional report of inconsistent recognition of Linux boot partitions by the Windows loader. There seems to be no hard-and-fast guideline as to which Windows installations will experience problems and which will not. The only certain way to know is to try it, and that requires patience, good backups, and a willingness to start over if it doesn't work.

So, if you are planning to use a dual or multiboot layout that includes Windows, and you don't have the time, patience, and determination to actually try all the alternatives, the answer comes down to the following practical considerations:

- Can you live without a major version upgrade to Internet Explorer?
- Can you run Windows as a VM instead of as part of a dual or multiboot system?
- Will your Windows bootloader recognize the Linux boot partition?

Many users never upgrade major versions of Internet Explorer, and are perfectly satisfied with security and feature updates to their current version. If this works for you, then proceed with the default placement in the MBR. If you absolutely must have the ability to upgrade major Internet Explorer versions, consider running Windows as a VM rather than as part of a dual or multiboot system. If you do not wish to do so (usually because of virtual hardware compatibility or licensing issues), then go with installing the Linux bootloader at the beginning of the Linux partition. Recent versions of Windows (since Vista) are pretty good about recognizing the Linux boot partition and adding it to the boot menu.

> Best practice is to use the default placement in the MBR. Only if you truly need the original bootloader should you place the Linux boot code at the beginning of the Linux boot partition and, if necessary, configure the non-Linux bootloader to include it in the boot menu, if it doesn't do so automatically.

Boot code under UEFI

The UEFI is a recent development by Intel and Microsoft that supports what is called Secure Boot, which requires all the loaded firmware to be signed or it won't be loaded. This is a problem for Linux, since the keys required for signing must, under the current GPL, be made public. This, of course, defeats the purpose. There are several workarounds, including some being used by Red Hat, SuSE, and Ubuntu, which are being discussed by the Debian developers and will probably be included in an update at some future point. For now, the UEFI specification allows Secure Boot to be disabled, and that is the recommended way to install Debian so that it boots under UEFI. It is also possible to switch on Legacy mode in most UEFI implementations, which allows the old MBR method to work as well.

Under UEFI, boot code is placed in a subdirectory in a special partition. Generally, this will be a subdirectory of `/EFI` in the first partition on the disk (formatted with the FAT32 filesystem). Generally, the boot modules and configuration files are placed in the `/EFI/grub` directory in the UEFI partition. It is not a good idea to replace the default EFI module (usually `/EFI/Boot/bootx64.efi`) by copying the `grubx64.efi` module over it, as some have recommended in the past. Debian installation generally takes care of including the GRUB loader as one of the options when booting, and if it isn't the default option, the boot settings menu should be used to set it as the default. It can also be used to add it as an option if the installation doesn't do this for you.

> Getting into the UEFI boot settings menu usually involves holding down certain keys while booting the computer, very similar to the way the old BIOS menus were invoked. It is different for each computer model.

UEFI is new to Debian 7.

Filesystem types

Selecting a filesystem format is the next major choice before installing Debian. The supported formats that are appropriate for a Linux installation include ext2, ext3, ext4, JFS, XFS, ReiserFS, and Btrfs. The first three are actually progressive versions of the **extended filesystem** (**ext**) developed specifically for Linux.

ext2, ext3, and ext4

The ext filesystem was originally developed to overcome the limitations of the MINIX filesystem.

> MINIX was Linus Torvalds' inspiration for Linux.

The **second extended filesystem** (**ext2**) improved upon it, while the **third extended filesystem** (**ext3**) added journaling, as well as performance improvements. The **fourth extended filesystem** (**ext4**) added additional features and performance improvements.

> The ability to disable journaling is one reason ext2 was sometimes used over ext3 for flash drives in order to reduce the write cycles.

Journaled File System

Developed by IBM for its Unix-like AIX operating system, and offered as an alternative to the ext and ext2 filesystems via release under the GPL, **Journaled File System** (**JFS**) is one of the alternatives to the current ext4. It uses fewer resources, while remaining quite stable and resilient. It includes many features of Btrfs, and is a good choice when CPU power is limited, or with database systems that require synchronous writes to survive hardware failures.

SGI's XFS File System

XFS is another alternative, developed by Silicon Graphics in 1993. It is a high-speed JFS, with emphasis on parallel **input/output** (**I/O**). The NASA Advanced Supercomputing Division uses this format on their 300+ terabyte Altix storage servers. Metadata operations are somewhat slower than other formats, although this was improved somewhat with the changes made by Red Hat. This is a good choice where metadata changes very little (such as few file or directory creation, move, or delete operations) and I/O performance is of utmost importance.

Reiser File System

Reiser File System (**ReiserFS**) was intended to supplant ext3 as the filesystem of choice for Linux, offering improved performance. At one point, ReiserFS version 3 was the default format choice for SuSE Linux. Version 4 was released, but development waned when the company went out of business, and SuSE eventually decided to go back to ext3 as its default.

ReiserFS offered some advantages over formats existing at the time, but it has fallen behind in some performance areas. It does support dynamic resizing, while other filesystems must be offline in order to be resized, or use a logical volume manager to provide virtual resizing support.

B-Tree File System

B-Tree File System (**Btrfs**) is the next Linux filesystem format. It focuses on fault-tolerance, repair, and easy administration, with the ability to scale up to larger storage configurations. ext-based systems can be easily converted to Btrfs. For the moment, Btrfs is still under heavy development, although only forward-compatible format changes are anticipated. Debian 7 does allow it to be used, but it is not yet recommended for production systems.

Clustered formats

There are various formats supported for clustered systems, including AFS and GFS2. In general, they are not used for the basic system files required for booting, but are better suited for shared data. It is possible to set up such systems for booting, but this is beyond the scope of this discussion. If you are interested, there are a number of publications available on Linux clustering. A good starting point might be the Wikipedia article on clustered filesystems at `http://en.wikipedia.org/wiki/Clustered_file_system`.

Non-Linux formats

The Linux kernel supports many additional formats, such as Microsoft's NTFS, the various FAT formats, the old OS/2 HPFS, and Apple's HFS. These formats do not support the attributes required by a Linux system, and are thus not appropriate for a root filesystem. They could be used for other data should it be necessary. Note that these formats lack the basic Linux security attributes, although there is some provision for translating the attributes that do exist into their approximate Linux equivalents.

Other Unix formats

Many other formats are available, such as SCO's Unix BFS, QNX, and BSD's UFS. Although Unix-related, they are not considered appropriate for Linux root installations due to slight differences in attribute handling. They may work fine, but the Linux-specific formats generally have better performance and features.

Choosing a format

Generally, the default ext4 format is the best choice. In specific cases, JFS or XFS may provide some advantages, and if the ability to resize dynamically is more important than performance or scalability, and you don't want to use logical volumes, ReiserFS (especially version 4) might be appropriate. Btrfs should not be used for critical data yet, but at some point soon it will become the preferred format. Non-Linux formats should not be used for the basic system.

Partitioning

The next decision to be made is how to partition the available storage space. There are the following three main considerations when deciding how to partition storage for a Debian system:

- Efficient backup and recovery
- Limiting space
- Disk management

Partitioning for backup and recovery

In the past, backups were performed on full partitions. Large partitions could take a long time to back up, and the system could not write to the partition during the process. With the advent of incremental and live backups, this is no longer a primary consideration. Another problem was that when a disk got corrupted, recovery usually was limited to a single partition. There are partition repair utilities now that can fix most problems (though not all), and only those files that can't be fixed need to be recovered.

Still, limiting the damage and the focus of recovery can be useful and remains a valid consideration.

Space-limiting partitions

Some administrators used partitions to limit the space available for certain directories. A good example is a mail spool directory. A massive spam attack can quickly consume large amounts of disk space. Using a separate partition for the spool directories will limit the total space that can be used by spool files, and the errors generated when no space remains alerts the administrator to the condition.

The availability of account quota systems for Linux can handle this situation without using partitions, but some administrators still prefer the hard limit of partitions.

Disk management

Aside from backup, recovery, and damage limitation, there are administrative functions that may differ depending on how a disk is partitioned. In particular, using a single partition for an entire disk relieves an administrator from having to modify partition sizes if one partition fills up and more space is necessary. This is frequently why a single disk partition (plus swap space) is the recommendation for new users who are uncertain how they want to partition their drives.

> Early BIOS systems could not boot from locations beyond the first 1024 cylinders of the disk. Thus, at one time, it was necessary to create a small/boot partition below that limit so that the system code (which could access larger areas) could be booted.

Logical Volume Management

Logical Volume Management, or **LVM**, is a format pretty much exclusive to Linux. It is an alternative to partitions which makes space management much easier. Logical volumes can be resized at will, and can span multiple disks. They can be migrated to different disks without interrupting services (live migration). There are also striping and mirroring features that are similar to RAID 0 and RAID 1.

LVM is more complex than basic partitioning, and not commonly used except in large storage installations.

> Technically, LVM is a structure that overlays the physical disk partitioning.

The swap partition

If available, a swap file or partition is used by Linux when memory paging to disk is necessary. With the advent of cheap memory, such paging is often infrequent with one exception: system hibernation. This is where the system is paused and the memory contents are written to disk prior to power off in order to allow the system to resume from the saved state. While this is commonly associated with laptop systems, servers sometimes make use of it as well.

Swap files are single files created within an existing filesystem, while swap partitions are exactly that—a specially formatted disk partition. In general, swap files are only used when additional swap space is necessary for some reason, as it has all the additional overhead (metadata, journaling, allocation, and such) of the filesystem in which it resides.

Unless an administrator is absolutely certain a system will never need to swap to disk or require the ability to hibernate, a swap partition equal in size to the installed memory is recommended.

> **Solid-state drives (SSD)**, so-called flash drives, were once considered an exception. In that the limited write cycles were considered a problem if swap files were placed on such a drive. However, with modern flash technology, this is no longer an issue, especially since the swapping has been greatly reduced by the large amounts of memory in current systems.

Selecting a partitioning scheme

The single partition (plus swap space) per disk scheme is the most common nowadays, as it is simple to create and manage. Multiple partitions may be used in the special cases mentioned previously, although, in general, the quality and speed of current backup utilities minimizes the need for separate partitions just for backup efficiency. If the system has multiple disks and may require resizing or live migration in the event of hardware changes, then LVM should be considered.

In general, the Debian defaults follow best practice. This usually means a single root partition and a single swap partition. If the administrator wants multiple partitions but isn't certain of the sizes required and doesn't want to use LVM, the defaults for the multipartition setup are a good starting point.

> An exception to accepting the single root and single swap partitions default is the case of disk encryption discussed later. If implemented via the Linux kernel, an unencrypted/boot partition is required.

Encryption

The final choice to be made prior to installation is whether to encrypt the disk contents. There are two main options, disk encryption and directory encryption.

> In some countries, encryption is subject to legal restrictions. Know the laws in your jurisdiction!

Why encrypt?

One of the main reasons for encryption is to keep private and sensitive data secure from unauthorized access. Laptops, for example, are frequently stolen and their contents have, in some well-publicized cases, been made public or put to harmful or illegal uses. Servers, on the other hand, aren't usually stolen, but they do have multiple users, and while the Linux permissions system can prevent unauthorized access, there are ways for hackers to bypass it, and they are constantly trying. For example, if one can gain root access, either legally as a system administrator, or illicitly by exploiting unpatched software security vulnerabilities, read/write access to everything on the system is allowed. Or, if a user is not careful with setting permissions, access via other users may be allowed unintentionally. In all cases, access by anyone who does not have the proper keys can be prevented by encryption.

Disk encryption

Disk encryption comes in several flavors. Full disk encryption, where the entire contents of the storage device are encrypted, is handled by hardware in the disk drive itself, or on the system's motherboard. This is because the code necessary to decrypt the disk can't really reside on the disk, since it will be in encrypted form and thus can't be loaded until decrypted. Since this method depends on the motherboard or disk software, which varies with manufacturer, it won't be covered here.

> A non-hardware method does exist, using an unencrypted USB stick or other media to provide the boot code, but requires special steps for creating the boot media that won't be covered here either.

Partial disk encryption, where individual partitions are encrypted, can be handled by Linux directly. There must be some unencrypted area from which the decryption software and keys can be loaded. This usually means an unencrypted boot partition, or booting from an unencrypted USB stick, thus getting the initial decryption software loaded and then chain loading from the encrypted disk. The keys themselves are encrypted by a password or pass phrase that is required at boot time to keep the keys secure.

A special case would be encrypting the swap partition. If there is any page swapping, or if hibernation (suspend to disk) is used, information in memory can be exposed to anyone who can read the partition. For this reason, many administrators encrypt the swap partition.

Disk encryption is appropriate for laptops, or for separate partitions on servers that contain sensitive data.

Directory encryption

An alternative to encrypting full partitions or disks is to encrypt portions of a filesystem, usually a directory and everything below it in the hierarchy, by using special features of Linux so that the encryption and decryption are handled automatically by the kernel or special software in the background. Thus, there are no implications for booting (as long as the boot directory isn't encrypted) and no installation issues, as it is configured after installation. Directory encryption is appropriate for servers containing sensitive information that resides in certain parts of the directory hierarchy.

Debian provides several packages for this type of encryption. The two most common are encfs and cryptsetup.

Choosing encryption

There are two primary disadvantages to disk or directory encryption. The first is probably the most serious; if the password is forgotten, the data is permanently lost and completely unrecoverable unless unencrypted backups (or encrypted backups where the password has not been lost) are available. The second disadvantage is performance. Most software encryption modules perform well, but there is no avoiding some overhead, even if it is minimal. Hardware encryption, such as that provided by the motherboard or the disk controller or drive itself, generally does not have significant overhead.

> Best practice is to evaluate whether the disadvantages of encryption outweigh the potential damage from compromised or stolen systems.
>
> In general, laptops with sensitive information and systems that contain sensitive information with many users, or that potentially can be accessed by hackers (such as web servers for example, which must be publicly accessible in order to serve their purpose) should use directory encryption at the very least. Disk encryption, especially if implemented in hardware, is even better.
>
> Most corporate policies require partial or full (if available) disk encryption on laptops, and directory encryption as a minimum on public servers.

Installing Debian

The actual installation is quite straightforward, and is considered one of the simplest distributions for base installs. Boot up the installation disk, and answer the necessary questions. A help button is frequently available to provide additional information during the installation. Also, standard and advanced installation subjects (including much of what is discussed in this chapter) are covered in detail in the Debian installation guide for the current release, available at `http://www.debian.org/releases/stable/installmanual`.

> Recommended practice is to install only the base system and use the package manager to install additional software after the system is up and running. However, it is possible during installation to select tasks which will install additional classes of software (such as the desktop environment which installs KDE, GNOME, XFCE, or LXDE, "Laptop" which installs software commonly used on laptops, and so on, all described in the installation guide). Doing this installs a standard set of additional software that suits most users' needs.

Summary

Prior to installing Debian, or any Linux distribution for that matter, an administrator should know whether he/she will be using single or dual/multiboot, and what his boot firmware is (BIOS or UEFI). It is also good to have some idea of where he/she will place the boot code, what filesystem types he/she will use, and some idea of his partitioning scheme. If unsure, the defaults offered by the Debian installer can be taken safely. If full disk encryption will be used, the setup depends on the hardware implementation and will probably need to be set up prior to installation. Directory encryption can be set up after the installation.

Once your system is set up, the next major issue to address is installing additional packages, which leads us to the next chapter on package management.

3
Package Management

You've installed a basic system, now it's time to install additional software. Or, if you've selected some tasks during installation, you want to see what's installed and maybe remove some you won't use. Maybe your boss has asked for a report on what's installed. Or what about security updates?

All of these, and more, are the province of the Debian package management system. In this chapter, we'll cover package managers, software selection and maintenance, how to update your system, and how to set up automatic updating.

> **A note for beginners**
>
> This section assumes that you are familiar with using the root account. Information on accessing root account functions is available at https://wiki.debian.org/Root, and in the Debian reference manual at http://www.debian.org/doc/manuals/debian-reference/. Quick help for commands mentioned in this chapter (as well as most Linux commands) can be obtained by executing man <command name> or info <command name> from the command line, or using the help button available in most graphical applications. The Debian reference manual also contains more detailed information on using the package manager commands in this chapter.

Package managers

The Debian package manager started out as a simple, command line utility, **dpkg**, with an additional utility called **dselect** that allowed more complex package selection and dependency resolution via a menu-based, curses interface. Eventually, additional utilities were developed to provide a better interface, better automatic dependency resolution, or both. The current standard package manager is Synaptic, a full-blown GUI application that runs in a graphical window manager, and provides extensive selection and reporting features.

We'll start at the beginning.

dpkg and dselect

These were the first package management tools for Debian. The `dpkg` command still does all of the work, since all the newer tools use it as a backend. As such, it has all the functions required to install, remove, configure, and report on packages. It is a command line tool.

One of the limitations of dpkg is that it does very little in the way of dependency checking, other than to offer an error message when there is a dependency problem. It requires the user to examine the dependency report and include the necessary packages during installation. Another limitation is that dpkg only works on packages that have already been downloaded. However, both of these limitations are addressed by the dselect utility.

The `dselect` command is a menu-driven utility that provides access to information on packages in the Debian repositories, and also checks and helps resolve software dependencies. This greatly simplifies package selection and installation. Once packages are selected and all dependencies satisfied, either automatically or with user assistance, `dpkg` is run automatically to perform the actual installation.

Advanced Package Tool

The **Advanced Package Tool** (**APT**) was developed to provide a better command line tool, that provides the download and dependency resolution of dselect without requiring a separate utility for installation. Think of it as an all-in-one command line tool that can select and install or remove packages, and automatically resolve dependencies.

APT is actually a set of utilities that include apt-get, the basic package installation tool, plus several other command line tools with an `apt` prefix that provide additional functions, such as reporting on available software, and other basic local repository maintenance functions.

> The `man apt` command is a good starting point, as it references other man pages for the additional commands. The Debian reference manual also has a lot of information on these and other package management commands

This tool is fast and, except in unusual circumstances, handles dependencies without requiring user intervention. It is the basic tool used for automatic, unattended software installation and updating.

aptitude

aptitude is a frontend for the APT suite of tools, with added functions that make it a little more like dselect, where it offers finer-grained dependency checking, and resolves dependencies with user assistance rather than autonomously. As such, it is sometimes more successful than dselect or apt-get in resolving dependencies in ways that require fewer major software changes. Like dselect, it is menu-driven (using the curses interface), with command line functions as well. Due to the user assistance sometimes required for dependency resolution, it is less suited to unattended or automatic software updating. However, it will frequently find simpler solutions, involving fewer changes, when compared to APT.

Synaptic

Synaptic is a package manager with a complete GUI interface and no command line capability. It offers most of the capabilities of aptitude along with many of the repository handling features of dselect. Like the menu-based dselect and aptitude utilities, it provides a software list divided into sections of interest, such as databases, development, editors, and many more, which allow an administrator to browse available software more effectively. It also has search functions which allow easy discovery of packages for specific purposes.

> Best practices are as follows:
>
> - For general use - Synaptic
> - For automated installation - APT
> - For dependency resolution in difficult cases - aptitude

Package selection and maintenance

Debian software is grouped together in a release. All of the software in a release is available as a set of purchased or downloaded media (CDs, DVDs, or new with Debian 7, Blue-ray Discs), or as individual packages grouped in an online repository. While dpkg works only on packages already downloaded (or on media mounted locally), the other package management utilities understand offline media, and local and remote repositories, which must be configured.

Configuring media or repositories

All of the configuration for media or repositories resides in `/etc/apt`, in a file called `sources.list` and any files in `/etc/apt/sources.list.d` with a `.list` extension. These files can be modified manually using your preferred editor, manipulated by various APT utilities such as `apt-add-repository` or `apt-spy`, or via a menu item in the Synaptic GUI. Details on how each method works are available in various man pages, such as those for `sources.list`, `apt-add-repository` and `apt-spy`, and so on, or in the help files for Synaptic. However, since they all depend on the same configuration files and format, the required entries are all similar.

Each line includes an indicator of whether the repository contains binary packages or source packages (from which binary packages can be built), the location of the repository, the identity of the release, and the sections from which software may be selected. Generally, an entry for the media from which you installed Debian has already been made during the installation process, along with an entry for the online repositories if they were used during installation as well.

All package sources are identified by a URI, described in the `sources.list` man page. The release is identified by its release name (such as **squeeze** for Debian 6, or **wheezy** for Debian 7) or by a generic term such as stable, which refers to whatever the current stable release is.

> The current Debian stable release is Debian 7, code named wheezy, released on 4 May, 2013. At the time of writing, stable is a synonym for wheezy. Debian releases are named in order to make the mirroring of various distributions easier. The code names to date are all taken from the movie *Toy Story*. This tradition apparently began in 1996 when Bruce Perens, who worked for Pixar at that time, took command of the Debian Project.

Taking all these together, a set of repositories as they might appear in `/etc/apt/sources.list` would look like the following:

```
# deb cdrom:[Debian GNU/Linux 7.0.0 "Wheezy" - Official amd64 \
  NETINST Binary-1 20130504-14:43]/ stable main
```

```
deb http://ftp.us.debian.org/debian/ wheezy main non-free contrib

deb-src http://ftp.us.debian.org/debian/ wheezy main non-free \
  contrib


deb http://security.debian.org/ wheezy/updates main contrib \
  non-free

deb-src http://security.debian.org/ wheezy/updates main contrib \
  non-free


# wheezy-updates, previously known as 'volatile'

deb http://ftp.us.debian.org/debian/ wheezy-updates main contrib \
  non-free

deb-src http://ftp.us.debian.org/debian/ wheezy-updates main \
  contrib non-free
```

> **Beginner's note**
>
> Some of the lines in the example are too long for the page and are split into two lines, using the common convention of adding a backslash (\) at the end of the first line to indicate it is continued. In reality, these lines should not be split in the APT sources configuration files.

Let's take the lines one at a time.

The first line begins with a `#`, meaning this entry is disabled. This entry was made by a network installation, wherein a minimal CD is mounted, and basic software is installed to allow the remainder of the software to be installed from online repositories as listed in the later lines. Only the main section is required, as shown at the end of the line.

The next two lines are for binaries (`deb`) and source packages (`deb-src`), to be obtained from an HTTP server (`http://ftp.us.debian.org/debian`). The release is wheezy, and all three sections—main, contrib, and non-free—will be available. Following the main repository lines are two lines for binary and source package updates. This is where security updates to the stable release are available.

> Even if you prefer to use media for the release, rather than online repositories, you should include the update repositories, as this is the only way to obtain security fixes that are released as necessary.

Finally, there is a comment, and two lines for what used to be called the 'volatile' repository, and is now just referred to by the release code name followed by `-updates`. This repository contains packages that are routinely updated throughout the life of the release, much more often than the security update repository. Packages that include virus definitions are examples of software included in this repository.

While the various methods of configuring the repositories have slight differences, the same basic information will be required, no matter which method you use. Also, since all of the utilities use the same configuration files and format, information entered, deleted, or modified by one method will be immediately visible to all of the utilities.

All of the previous lines were pre-configured by the installation procedure, and did not need to be modified. However, there are often reasons to modify or add repositories. You may want to add repositories for software that isn't available directly from Debian, or modify the URL to use a different, better performing server, or different access method.

> For example, HTTP is more resistant to network delays or error, while FTP is somewhat faster. Also, not all mirrors support both methods, so if you change servers, you may need to change the access method as well.

There are a number of non-Debian repositories that contain software that is not included in the standard Debian release. Usually, this is due to licensing issues, or because development takes place outside of the Debian Project policies and there is no sponsor to integrate it into Debian. Some of the more useful ones are as follows:

- **Deb Multimedia**: As it says, this is primarily a multimedia package that can't be included in the normal distribution
- **Webmin**: This is a web-based system administration software
- **Oracle**: This provides Oracle Express software
- **Skype**: This provides the Skype software
- **MongoDB**: This is a software from the NoSQL MongoDB project

As an example, the following is a `/etc/apt/sources.list.d/webmin.list` file for the Webmin archive just mentioned:

```
deb http://download.webmin.com/download/repository sarge contrib
deb http://webmin.mirror.somersettechsolutions.co.uk/repository \
  sarge contrib
```

Generally, sites that offer such repositories will include instructions for configuring the sources list file for their repository.

The significance of the release name

One of the more subtle changes often made, other than adding non-Debian repositories, has very important implications. Note that the release name in most of the lines from the previous Debian release `sources.list` is wheezy. This means that the packages available through the package managers will always be from the Debian 7 release. Some administrators change the release name to stable. This has both advantages and disadvantages.

One advantage is that, when a new major version is released, your package managers will immediately recognize this and update package lists and dependencies accordingly. The disadvantage related is that major releases involve major changes in package dependencies. While package managers can handle this, such major changes usually result in many new packages being installed to satisfy new dependencies, many old ones being deleted due to changing dependencies or obsolescence, and major version changes that often change the way the software behaves. These changes can be quite disruptive to server operation, or to developers' or users' habits.

> Best practice to ensure stability is to leave the official release name in place until you are ready to upgrade to the next release. Then change the name in the package manager configuration, and perform a manual upgrade.

Selecting packages

Once you have the repositories that you want configured, you need to retrieve information about what is in the repositories. This includes not only package lists, but package descriptions, contents, and dependencies. This is done by updating your package cache, after which you can browse, select, install, upgrade, and delete packages.

Updating your package cache

The package information is updated simply by the refresh menu entry in Synaptic, or the aptitude or apt-get `update` command to update the package information cache. This should be done regularly to ensure that the information you have on available packages is current. Once you have the repositories configured and have updated the package information cache, you can select and install software from any or all of them as desired. There are two basic methods for selecting packages. command line and selection lists.

Command-line selection

This is the simplest and fastest method to install one or a few packages and their dependencies, but it requires that you know what packages you want to install. There are several utilities that can be used to search package names and descriptions, which will provide you with the means to find the proper package names. The most common of these is `apt-cache`. Once you know what package or packages you want to install, you can use apt-get or the command line format of aptitude or dselect to quickly download and install the packages.

Selection lists

Both aptitude and dselect provide a basic, interactive interface as well. You can navigate through a list of available packages, classified according to sections, or you can search for packages using a number of criteria. The interface is based on the simple curses library, and can seem cumbersome at times, although it is an improvement over the command line utilities mentioned previously. One advantage of these interfaces (as well as the command line utilities) is that they can be used in a terminal environment and do not require a graphic desktop environment be installed. They are frequently used on high-performance servers where a graphic desktop environment is not installed for security or performance reasons.

On the other hand, Synaptic provides a full GUI interface for browsing, searching, and selecting packages, as well as configuring repositories, selecting installation options, and providing information on available and installed packages. It requires a graphic desktop environment, such as GNOME or KDE, in order to operate.

> Synaptic can be run remotely, over a Secure Shell connection, from a system that does have a graphic window manager installed. Some administrators install Synaptic on servers without graphical desktops and use it in this manner to avoid security or performance issues of graphic environments on the server itself.

Meta packages

One of the most useful package types is called **meta packages**. These are packages that contain no software themselves, but that require other packages to be installed, and thus provide a unified set of software for a particular purpose. This works because, although no actual software is in the meta package, the package manager will select and install all of the required dependent packages, providing a complete set of features in a single, easy installation step.

Frequently, there are multiple packages with slightly different names that install a slightly different set of dependencies. A good example is GNOME. You can install the GNOME meta package, which will provide a complete GNOME installation, including many extras. Or, you can elect to install `gnome-core`, which provides only the basic desktop environment, and select from any of the additional packages that provide additional features and functions, such as:

- evolution (e-mail software, similar to Outlook)
- gnome-documents (document management features)
- gnome-games
- gnome-media (multimedia applications)
- libreoffice-gnome (office suite) and others

One minor problem with meta packages is that there is no easy way to search for them. Many do have 'meta' in their descriptions, which can facilitate some searches, but this is not universally true. The GNOME packages mentioned previously do not follow this convention as of Debian 7. Nevertheless, they are often fairly obvious, and not too difficult to find.

A word about dependency resolution

dselect, APT, aptitude, and Synaptic, all provide some form of automatic dependency resolution. In rare cases, a dependency can't be resolved automatically, and user intervention is required. aptitude will calculate alternatives and ask the user to select from them. APT and Synaptic generally require the user to add packages to the command line or selection list manually.

Such problems generally only occur in the testing and unstable releases, where software dependencies are constantly updated and some may not completely resolve until all of the software involved has been updated and placed in the release. However, one common source of this problem occurs in the stable release as well, and is due to a dependency on a **virtual package**.

A virtual package is not the name of an actual package, but the name of a library or function that any one of a number of packages can provide. Since there are usually multiple packages that can satisfy the dependency, the user must choose one to manually install, after which the remainder of the original dependencies can be satisfied automatically. This rarely occurs during a standard upgrade, and almost never during a distribution upgrade, where such virtual packages are selected automatically.

> In general, you will only see this problem, and then rarely, when installing single packages manually.

Removing packages

Removing packages is also handled by any of the package managers. Something to be aware of, however, is that apt-get and Synaptic do not automatically remove dependencies after the package that depends on them is removed. The command `apt-get autoremove` should be used to do this, no matter which package manager was used for installation and removal. aptitude does this automatically.

Keeping current

After installing the software you need for your system, it is good practice to check for updates at regular intervals. In particular, security updates are released as soon as possible after a security flaw in any Debian software is identified.

It is easy to update a Debian system. After updating the package cache (see the previous section on *Updating your package cache*) so that it holds current information on all software in the repositories, the Synaptic mark all upgrades menu item, or the apt-get or aptitude `upgrade` command will update all software with any newer versions available.

Automatic updates

It is possible to perform automatic, unattended updates to a system, but there are some potential problems. Setting it up is quite simple. Just install the unattended-upgrades package. If you aren't asked during installation if you want to enable automatic security upgrades, run the command `dpkg-reconfigure -plow unattended-upgrades`.

Generally, only security upgrades will be automatically installed, which will minimize potential problems, which include modified dependencies and changes that modify how the software is configured or how it operates. It is possible to allow other upgrades by modifying the configuration file in `/etc/apt/apt.conf.d/50unattended-upgrades`. The file is commented to help identify the modifications desired, generally just removing the // in front of the lines you want to enable. Note that enabling anything other than security updates can result in errors (when dependency issues are encountered) or system disruption (when the upgrade modifies software behavior or configuration). This is especially true if the stable release name is used, which can result in very major changes when a new stable version is released.

[Best practice is to allow automatic installation of security upgrades only (use the default configuration). The package information cache for all packages will be updated in any case, so you can manually upgrade the rest of the packages periodically, allowing you to address any unusual upgrade issues as they arise.]

Foreign packages

What do you do when a package doesn't exist in Debian? There are several options. One mentioned previously is to add non-Debian repositories to the repository configuration. After a Synaptic refresh, apt-get, or aptitude `update`, all of the package information in the repository will be available to the Debian package managers.

If, however, the software isn't included in any repository, there are a couple of options available.

[There is actually one additional option: just install such software from its original source. This technique is not recommended because it places the software completely outside of the package management system. Future system upgrades that involve required libraries can cause the software to behave strangely or even break completely, and finding the reason can be quite frustrating. This technique should be used as a last resort only.]

Alien

If the package exists in some other Linux distribution, it can often be converted to a Debian package. This is done using a package called **alien**. Alien provides commands to convert between a number of package formats (including Red Hat RPM, Stampede SLP, Slackware TGZ, Solaris PKG, and Debian DEB).

[Before using alien, note the warnings in the man page.]

In general, the conversion itself is fairly straightforward. Although the results cannot be guaranteed, the converted package often will install okay under Debian. Any problems that do occur are most likely to be caused by different library dependency names, or even differences in software level identification.

All is not lost when this happens, however. Alien can perform a partial conversion, essentially stopping at the point where it has created the temporary directory from which it normally builds the Debian package. You can then go into the directory and make the necessary modifications, and then complete the build manually.

Manual builds

It is also possible to build Debian packages yourself, either from a partial alien conversion (as previously discussed), or from scratch using the original software. The procedure can vary from simple to complex, depending on what the package is to provide, and is well covered in the Debian maintainer's guide and the Debian policy manual, both available online or as installable packages in Debian, and in many other online resources. A good online starting place is the Debian packaging Wiki page at `https://wiki.debian.org/HowToPackageForDebian`.

> Manual builds, either from scratch or from a partial alien conversion, are the recommended way to handle software that cannot be obtained in standard Debian format.

Details vary greatly, depending on the actual software involved. Generally, a package is built from source code, but it is also possible to build a package from a binary only software release as well. The general procedure for this is as follows:

1. Obtain the source (or binary files) and place in an appropriate package building directory.
2. Create the necessary Debian packaging files, which include additional documentation as necessary, optional script files specific to Debian packages, files to control the package building process, and files required by Debian package managers.
3. Test the build. If necessary, add patches to correct any problems in packaging, or that are required for the software to compile or run properly in a Debian environment.
4. Repeat steps 2 and 3 until the final product installs and runs on your distribution.

The packages available to Debian developers are included in the distribution for anyone to use. The primary ones used in building your own packages are:

- build-essential (packages essential for building Debian packages)
- dpkg-dev (package development tools)
- fakeroot (allows users to build as if they were the root user)

- dh-make (tools to create files in the debian package build directory)
- debhelper (helper programs for the debian/rules file)
- cdbs (optional, additional helper programs for the debian/rules file)
- quilt (debian package patch management)

It is all but impossible to give any general example, as every package will differ in all but the first step. However, there are many good examples and tutorials available online, and the full package source of all Debian packages included in the distribution is available for anyone to examine and learn from.

Upgrading your system

As mentioned previously, it is simple to update your system. The commands (or menu items) for upgrading your system to the next official release are different from the standard updating commands. The apt-get command `dist-upgrade` or the aptitude `full-upgrade` will perform the necessary special calculations to upgrade to the next major distribution release after the package information cache has been updated (either using the normal `update` command if you have configured the release name as stable, or after changing to the new release name and executing the `update` command). The reason for the special commands is that there are major changes in package dependencies between official releases, and the way some software is configured, as well as the removal of obsolete packages, all of which require special calculations not involved in a normal package upgrade.

> Synaptic can also handle a full distribution upgrade, but instead of a different command, it handles such upgrades when 'smart upgrade' is set in Preferences instead of 'default upgrade'.

Prior to the upgrade

Read the release notes! This can't be emphasized enough. The Debian developers are careful to include all the important details on what has changed between releases, and any special steps required prior to and after the upgrade process.

There are two ways to handle a major upgrade: all-at-once, and a little at a time (which we'll refer to as a partial upgrade). The all-at-once upgrade basically involves a single command that updates all packages. The partial upgrade method involves selecting a group of packages and updating them and their dependencies. This reduces the dependency calculations to a more easily handled subset. Generally, one selects one of the meta packages, such as GNOME or Apache2, or a selected set of packages to update, and uses the `install` command in either apt-get or aptitude, or selects the packages in dselect, aptitude, or Synaptic. After they are upgraded, the next set is chosen and updated, until all packages have been updated, along with any new dependencies or removals required. At some point, after the majority of software has been upgraded, the remainder of the upgrade can be handled all at once.

Choosing a subset of packages is fairly simple. The apt-get `dist-upgrade` command and aptitude `full-upgrade` command will provide information on what will be added, upgraded, and removed and ask you to confirm the selection. At this point, you can tell them not to perform the upgrade, then review the packages proposed for upgrading, and select one or a few to use with the apt-get or aptitude command line `install` command (which upgrades already installed packages). A similar procedure works with Synaptic.

> One way to ease the upgrade process is to perform a standard package upgrade first. This will perform the simpler, standard package upgrades that don't require major changes in dependencies. Once this is done, the full distribution upgrade will involve fewer packages

During the upgrade

You've selected the packages to upgrade (or are performing an all at once upgrade), and started the process. The first thing to note is what packages are going to be removed. If one or more of them appear to be packages you need, cross-check them with the packages being installed to see if they are being replaced by a new package with similar functions. If they are not, make a note to follow the upgrade with a separate installation of whatever packages are required.

During a distribution upgrade, the system can generally remain in operation, although there will be slight disruptions when a package requires certain services to be restarted or libraries to be loaded.

> These disruptions are more severe than a normal upgrade, particularly in cases where a package is removed and replaced with a different one to fulfill the same function, or removed because it is obsolete. Therefore, you may want to inform users prior to the upgrade, and keep system activity to a minimum.

The next thing to watch for is the upgrade notes. Major changes are in how some software works are displayed (and e-mailed to the root account for later checking as well) in order to notify the installer of necessary post-installation steps to be taken.

Finally, when the administrator has made changes to the configuration of a package, the upgrade process will notify him/her of the non-default configuration and ask for help in resolving the differences. This involves leaving the current local version in place, replacing it with the developers' version, or pausing the installation so the differences can be examined and resolved manually.

> Often there are new options or defaults that should be added to the old configuration. Best practice is to either resolve the changes immediately, or keep the old configuration and cross-check it later with the new default configuration (which is placed in the same directory with a modified name to keep it inactive but available for just this reason).

After the upgrade

Once the distribution upgrade is complete, there are still a few steps that should be taken. First, if the configuration file issues weren't resolved during installation, now is the time to do this. The new file is in the same place as the old one, with an added `dpkg-new` extension. If the installer selected the developers' version, the old configuration is there with a `dpkg-old` extension. Either way, the administrator can check them for differences and make the necessary changes.

Next, if there are major changes in software operation, any applications that use the software should be modified, or the configuration updated to recreate the old behavior if possible. A good example of this issue is major changes to how PHP works, which often necessitates re-coding web pages that used the changed features or modifying the configuration when it supports operation in a legacy mode. Other major changes may affect users, such as the change from GNOME 2 to GNOME 3, which involves a major change in the user experience. Also, any post-installation steps noted in the release notes should be taken.

Summary

The package managers in Debian make it easy to upgrade software packages, and even upgrade to a new, major release level. Upgrades don't require major server downtime, although if they involve major software changes that modify how the software is configured or behaves, additional work may be required after the upgrade to return service to normal. Non-Debian repositories can be added so that the package managers can update non-Debian software just as easily as official Debian packages. If software isn't available in Debian format, it can be packaged using the same tools Debian developers use, so that Debian package managers will handle it as well.

Usually after an installation or upgrade, there are additional steps that must be taken. The major one is package configuration, which we will cover in the next chapter.

4
Basic Package Configuration

Debian depends heavily on the configuration methods used by the upstream developers of each package, supplemented by the Debian developers' modifications and additions to standardize package configuration, and make the administrator's life easier. In this chapter, we will cover the standard location of configuration files, utilities available to assist in configuration, trends in configuration file management, and some examples.

Configuration files

Most configuration files reside in the `/etc` directory hierarchy. In general, most packages place their configuration files in a subdirectory named after the software. In cases where the upstream developers do not do this, the Debian package usually modifies the behavior. A good example is the **BIND** DNS server software. Traditionally, the base configuration is placed in `/etc/named.conf`, with any other configuration files placed in the `/var/lib/named` directory. The Debian BIND package places all configuration files in `/etc/bind9` and its subdirectory.

In addition, there is a `/etc/`default directory, in which commonly modified options are placed in a file matching the package name. Again, using BIND, the file is `/etc/default/bind9`, and contains two simple options: whether the `resolvconf` dynamic resolver is being used, and what options the server should be run with. We'll cover this directory first.

/etc/default

The configuration files in this directory are intended to control the standard initialization scripts found in /etc/init.d (known as init scripts), or the way various system libraries behave. They contain environment variable definitions that are used by system libraries or in the init scripts, to control execution options, software module loading, and anything else that can be controlled dynamically.

In the case of definitions used by the init scripts, the variables usually include a definition of command line options to be used. In some cases, setting one of the variables modifies the behavior of the script. For example, setting RESOLVCONF to anything but no in /etc/default/bind9 will cause the init script to use the resolvconf utility to add an appropriate resolver line for the local loopback interface during initialization (and remove it during shutdown).

For those scripts that apply to system libraries, they generally define default behavior for commands or software that the libraries affect. A good example of this is /etc/default/nss, which controls how the **Name Service Switch** (**NSS**) functions in the GNU C library. In particular, it controls what information the library will consider authoritative for NSS calls, as well as the behavior of certain function calls.

> In special cases, the default definition file may not be a single file, but a subdirectory of /etc/default. This is done to split information into groups of related variables, both for ease of update, and to allow local modifications that won't be overwritten when configuration files are replaced.

/etc/<package name>

Configuration files are placed in /etc by most software developers, and this is standard practice for Debian packages. If the file is fairly simple, and the only file required, it is often placed directly in /etc with a .conf extension, such as /etc/inetd.conf for the openbsd-inetd package. For packages that require a more complex configuration, usually via multiple configuration files, those files are placed in a subdirectory of /etc which is generally named after the package. A good example of this is the apache2 package, which has its configuration files in /etc/apache2 and its subdirectories.

Multiple files in a subdirectory are used for a number of reasons. In some cases, it is because the original software uses different files for different purposes. In other cases, it is done to organize configuration items into a more manageable and understandable group. Occasionally, Debian developers have modified the package to organize the configuration to simplify or streamline administration.

A good example of this is Apache. Normal Apache configuration is either by a single file or multiple files that are included by the master configuration file. Traditionally, **SSL** (**Secure Sockets Layer**) certificates and keys, and Virtual Host configuration files are contained in subdirectory, but all major options are configured in one or a few files in the main directory. Debian has actually split the configuration into many files in various subdirectories. This allows Debian to supply separate packages that provide certain features via individual configuration files that are added to the proper directory, rather than requiring modification of the primary configuration files. Also, there are subdirectories for modules and virtual hosts prefixed by `available-` or `enabled-`. This allows a simple script to activate or deactivate modules and virtual hosts easily and quickly.

> As it's not yet available in the stable release, Debian developers are taking this concept further in future releases, by providing a config-available and config-enabled directory, as well as allowing features to be activated and deactivated without editing config files or installing or removing feature packages. This will probably be available in Debian 8, code-named **Jessie**.

Initial configuration

One of the stability requirements for Debian is that when a package is installed, it should not adversely affect the system. Often, this is as simple as providing a standard configuration, such as Apache's simple **It works!** page. In other cases, however, at least some information must be provided during installation in order to create a basic, working configuration. This is handled by having the installation procedure ask the necessary questions during the installation process in order to create a working configuration. In fact, Debian developers have created the extensive `debconf` subsystem for this purpose.

The `debconf` subsystem provides the ability to configure packages before, during, and after installation, and it is integrated into all Debian packages that require configuration. It supports a number of frontend user interfaces, prewritten answers that can be input to the installation process, a simple interface for asking questions and providing the answers to the installation scripts, and even ways to reconfigure packages any time after installation. In general, this method of configuration provides only the most commonly used configuration options. More complex configurations must be handled by using any utilities provided by the packages, or by editing the configuration files directly.

Even if you edit configuration files directly, Debian administrators have passed on various techniques to the developers to ease this process. In some cases, they have created alternative and more understandable configuration files that are scanned and used to create the actual, complex configuration by scripts provided in the package. A good example of this is the GRUB2 boot loader. An administrator makes whatever modifications to the configuration files in `/etc/default` and `/etc/grub.d`, and then runs `update-grub` to create the actual file that GRUB uses to load the operating system. The script then executes the necessary commands for creating and installing the configuration, as well as the necessary updates of other files affected by GRUB reconfiguration. This is just one example of how various utilities created by the Debian developers and other third parties have simplified Debian administration.

Another good example is sendmail. Administrators often modify the files and various database files required by sendmail to tailor it for large, corporate installations. However, instead of compiling the configuration and databases, then forcing sendmail to load the new configuration, a single command, `sendmailconfig`, will perform all of the necessary steps at once, with minimal interruption in server operation.

Configuration utilities

So, what are some of the utilities provided for Debian administration? We've already mentioned a couple of specialized ones for GRUB and sendmail. There are many others that handle specific software or services, either included in the Debian package itself, or in a separate package. Here, however, we're concerned with more general utilities. The two main ones are `dpkg-reconfigure` and `gadmin`.

dpkg-reconfigure

This utility reruns the same configuration scripts that run during installation. It is run from the command line, and options can be used to vary the level of complexity of the questions asked. It is generally used when extensive, local modifications aren't required and the administrator just wants to update the basic configuration as provided by the installation scripts. It is also useful if the basic configuration has been corrupted, or changes made that have caused the package to stop working, to return it to the configuration provided immediately after installation.

It is generally not useful if the configuration requires options that are not commonly used, or if the configuration requires extensive local modifications that aren't normally covered by the installation scripts, except perhaps to return the configuration to a post-installation condition as noted previously.

gadmin

This is actually a suite of packages, each covering a different major service. Unfortunately, this is not as universal as `dpkg-reconfigure`, but it does handle more complex configurations. The following services are covered as of Debian 7:

- Bind (DNS)
- OpenVPN (both client and server)
- ProFTPD (FTP)
- RSYNC
- Samba (Windows Shares)

It is a graphical tool, based on **GTK** (**GIMP Tool Kit**). It was developed to provide some administrator functions under the GNOME desktop environment. It will handle fairly complex configurations.

Desktop configuration

So far, we have been discussing server configuration. User configuration of a desktop environment is actually a little easier, as both **GNOME** (**GNU Object Model Environment**) and **KDE** (**K Desktop Environment**), as well as other desktop managers, provide a full suite of utilities gathered in one menu area that allows the user to easily configure things such as desktop appearance, behavior, window themes, login behavior, and system and session services relevant to their environment.

Other utilities

Finally, there are a number of packages that were created for the express purpose of configuring individual services. There are software packages that provide graphic or command line configuration tools for any number of other software packages. The packages vary in complexity and usage, as they are usually provided by third parties. They can be found by using any of the search capable Debian package managers. **Synaptic** is probably the easiest as it allows one to easily browse descriptions after searching.

> Many of the third-party utilities are not aware of modifications Debian makes to the configuration file layout in order to ease administration, upgrades, and stability. Often, they use the upstream configuration file layout, or sometimes even the author's idea of a better layout. Although the Debian package upgrade procedure will handle this as a local configuration file modification, it does make extra work for the administrator during upgrades. Keep this in mind when deciding whether to use third-party configuration utilities.

The next section will cover the preferred methods for local configuration in Debian.

Local configuration trends

Because Debian upgrades often affect configuration files, the developers have crafted techniques to lower the impact of upgrades on locally modified configurations. In particular, they are moving to provide separate local configuration files and special directories that help maintain local changes during upgrades.

Local configuration files

Many software packages are moving to a multiple file configuration system. Debian developers are using this feature to protect local changes by instructing administrators to place their modifications in a file with a `.local` extension. In other cases, such as the Apache configuration directories, files are placed in specified subdirectories (`conf.d` and `sites-available` in this case), and may be named freely, as long as they don't conflict with file names used by standard Debian or upstream configurations. In these cases, the Debian developers have modified the configuration files so they contain commands to include local configuration files, overriding the standard files as necessary. In any case, a savvy administrator will use such separate files for local configuration changes when possible, so that they are unaffected by package updates.

One of the side effects of this separation of local configuration files is that the update procedure will no longer ask you whether to install the developers' configuration, leave the local configuration, or reconcile the two. Generally, this is what you want, as your local changes will remain in place, and any new features will have reasonable defaults that shouldn't cause problems. However, in cases where there are possible major changes to the configuration defaults, a pop-up description of the changes occurs during the upgrade (requiring acknowledgement), and is also emailed to the root account. Even without this, though, it is good practice to browse the package documentation for configuration advice and the configuration files for any obvious changes, after the upgrade is complete.

Configuration subdirectories

Many software packages not only support separate, local configuration files, but also provide a special subdirectory to help organize and manage multiple configuration files. In some cases, the files in these directories require a specific extension in order to be considered active or enabled. This makes it easy to enable or disable software features. In other cases, all files in the directory are considered as part of the configuration, and a different method is used to enable and disable specific files or features, such as used in the Debian Apache software packages.

In any case, Debian developers usually recommend care in adding your own files, usually by including the word local somewhere in the name, or by placing them in directories that are provided specifically for local files.

Configuration advice

So, how do you know what configuration facilities are provided and what the recommended approach to local configuration is? The best place to begin is the `README.debian` file that comes with the package. It is a requirement of the **Debian Policy** manual that this file explains any special configuration issues, how configuration under Debian differs from the configuration provisions of the original software developers, and recommended ways to handle local configuration. It also explains any utilities Debian has added to aid in software configuration. This file exists in `/usr/share/doc/<package name>`, which also contains any original software documentation, plus any added by the Debian developers. This directory is standard with nearly all Debian packages, and is mandatory for any that have extensive documentation or special configuration issues.

> Some packages have such extensive documentation that it is provided in a separate package so that it can be installed on a separate system providing faster, local access to the information without requiring space or processing on the server on which the software is installed.

Let's take a look at some examples that involve fairly complex configuration file sets.

Apache configuration

Here we will look at the Apache web server software configuration and see how Debian handles it. The details on what the configuration actually does will not be covered, as they are complex and covered in the package documentation. However, we will look at how the files are set up, and what procedures are provided by Debian for configuration maintenance.

The first thing to observe about the Debian Apache packages is that the type of server, threaded, non-threaded, event-driven, or multi-user, is determined by which package is installed to satisfy the server dependency in the main apache2 meta package. In addition, the documentation is split off into a separate package, which places the Apache manuals in a web directory and adds the necessary configuration files so that Apache can serve them up as web pages.

Configuration files

The basic configuration file layout is as follows and is also documented in the `/etc/apache2/apache2.conf`:

```
/etc/apache2/
|-- apache2.conf
|        `--  ports.conf
|-- mods-enabled
|        |-- *.load
|        `-- *.conf
|-- conf.d
|        `-- *
`-- sites-enabled
         `-- *
```

The files shown are the only ones that are considered part of the actual apache2 configuration by virtue of being included by commands in the main configuration file or one of the files it includes. Note that there is also a `sites-available` and a `mods-available` directory that are not automatically included in the configuration. The files in these latter two directories are included by virtue of links pointing to them from the `mods-enabled` and `sites-enabled` directories, which we will cover shortly.

In general, configuration changes will be limited to the `ports.conf` file, adding or modifying files in `conf.d`, and the links in `mods-enabled` and `sites-enabled` directories (and the files they point to). Any files you modify that are provided as part of one of the Debian packages will, of course, be checked during upgrades and you will be prompted for the proper action. Such files are generally only:

- `envvars`: This is the file containing environment variables used by Apache and the `apache2ctl` utility
- `ports.conf`: This is the file that controls which ports and IP addresses Apache listens on
- `.conf` extension files in `mods-available` directory: These are the files which control the configuration of a module when loaded

- `default` and `default-ssl` in `sites-available` directory: These are the files which control the behavior of the default web service
- files in the `conf.d` directory: These are the files that are part of add-on packages, such as `phpmyadmin`

Modifications to these files should, of course, be kept to a minimum, but sometimes they are necessary. Most local configuration will be done by adding files to the `conf.d` directory, or to the `sites-available` directory (along with appropriate links in the `sites-enabled` directory), where virtual hosts are configured.

> In Debian 7, the files are only included if they begin with a letter or number. It does not include `.dpkg` and do not contain anything other than letters, numbers, and underscores. In Debian 8, only files that end in `.conf` or `.load` will be included.

Enabling sites and modules

As mentioned previously, site and module configurations and options are placed in the `sites-available` and `mods-available` directories. They are not included unless there is a link to them in the `sites-enabled` or `mods-enabled` directory. Instead of making the links manually, use the `a2enmod` and `a2dismod` commands to enable or disable modules, and the `a2ensite` and `a2dissite` commands to enable or disable specific site configurations.

Testing and activating the configuration

Once all modifications have been made, and the appropriate sites or modules enabled, it is best to test the configuration for obvious errors. While it is possible to use the `init` script in `/etc/init.d/apache2` for this, the `apache2ctl` utility is specifically intended for, and better suited for this purpose. There is a `configtest` command option (detailed in the `apache2ctl` manual page) which will perform basic checking on all of the included files. It won't catch all errors, but it will catch the majority of them. After you are confident the configuration is correct, it is necessary to reload or restart Apache in order for the changes to become effective. Again, while the `init` script can handle this, using `apache2ctl` is the preferred method.

There are two ways to get Apache to reload its configuration files, a regular restart, or a graceful restart (which doesn't actually restart, it just reloads the configuration). The graceful restart is the preferred method because if there is some issue with the configuration, especially something the `configtest` was unable to catch, the web service continues running with the old configuration, avoiding server downtime while you fix the problem. A graceful restart may take some time if there are long-running threads, since it waits until all threads are idle before reloading the configuration. A full restart forcibly terminates all threads and reloads the configuration, and won't restart the server after it is fully stopped, if there are configuration errors.

Other examples

The Apache example should give you a feel for how Debian splits configuration files into smaller, more easily managed files, and provides means to ease various administration tasks, such as activating and deactivation modules. Other software will have different layouts, as well as, different configuration features and utilities, all described in the appropriate documentation.

Exim, for example, uses a single, monolithic configuration file. In order to split files out, Debian provides a utility `update-exim4.conf` that combines all of the separate configuration files from the `/etc/exim4/conf.d` hierarchy into the single file required by the exim4 software. There are several minor variations in how this may be done (all explained in the documentation), so that an administrator can choose his preferred method.

Debian sendmail, another email package, uses another method. All of its configuration files are in the `/etc/mail` hierarchy, and **GNU make** is used after updating the configuration to create all of the necessary database and config files. In fact, a special utility, `sendmailconfig`, will not only run make for you, it will also handle incorporating `/etc/default/sendmail` changes, and reload the sendmail configuration after processing is complete.

All of this shows how the Debian developers provide various methods of making configuration easier. Simpler packages may have few, one, or no configuration files. Those with larger or more complex configuration won't all be handled identically, although the technique of splitting files into smaller, easier to modify pieces and providing utilities to ease config administration will be common to most (and, per Debian policy, described in the documentation for each package).

Summary

Although Debian stays close to the upstream software developer's configuration methods, the Debian developers frequently modify configuration file layout to simplify local configuration and upgrades, and often provide additional utilities to ease the administrator's job. Third-party utilities are sometimes available as well, but the administrator should understand that the output of these utilities may not always follow the Debian configuration layout.

Now, with basic software configuration out of the way, it's time to cover more system wide administration issues.

5
System Management

Aside from configuring individual software packages, an administrator is responsible for managing how the various services on his systems are started and stopped, managing network connections, maintaining the filesystem, managing system logs, and configuring the face the system shows to the users.

Startup and shutdown

The proper startup and shutdown of services required for a system to function and fulfill its purpose is central to its management. While Unix `init` scripts (also known as System V or SysV scripts, due to their origin in Unix System V) have a long history and are in one form or another, common to all Unix and Linux systems, the way in which they are managed, sequenced, enabled, disabled, and the preferred script format often differs somewhat between distributions. The primary areas to be aware of for Debian startup and shutdown scripts include the purpose of run levels, dependency-based sequencing, and utilities available for administering the boot sequence.

Debian run levels

In Debian, as in nearly all Unix/Linux operating systems, run levels from 0 through 6 are available, defined as follows:

- 0: System Halt
- 1: Single User (maintenance)
- 2 to 5: Multi-User Modes
- 6: System Reboot

Note that run levels 2 through 5 are identical in Debian. This is unlike some other distributions, such as RedHat, Fedora, SuSE, or OpenSuSE, which give specific purposes to some of these run levels. For example, run level 2 in these distributions is often defined as one without network support, 3 with networking, 4 with file sharing, and 5 includes a display manager which isn't active in the other run levels.

In most Debian systems, there is no difference between the multiuser run levels, and all of the `init` scripts default to active in levels 2 through 5. This doesn't mean you can't define your own purposes for different run levels. However, if you do choose to do this, do not manually edit the various links to `init` scripts in the run level directories. The `update-rc.d` command should be used instead. The reason for this is that Debian now defaults to dependency based boot sequencing.

Dependency-based boot sequence

As mentioned previously, this is now the default as of Debian 7 Wheezy. It was introduced in Debian 6 Squeeze, although it could be turned off. It is now always enabled, although provisions are made for legacy ordering (assigning specific numbers to start and stop scripts). Because of this, the administrator no longer needs to determine the order in which the `init` scripts are run. This is now handled by the `insserv` utility.

> The `insserv` utility should not be called directly. The `update-rc.d` utility provided by Debian, which calls the low-level `insserv` command, is the recommended interface to manage `init` scripts.

The `init` scripts must now have dependencies and defaults listed in a special set of headers, along with a description of the script, what service or services it provides, and what run levels the service should be active in. A good example is the beginning of the script for starting Apache:

```
#!/bin/sh
### BEGIN INIT INFO
# Provides:          apache2
# Required-Start:    $local_fs $remote_fs $network $syslog $named
# Required-Stop:     $local_fs $remote_fs $network $syslog $named
# Default-Start:     2 3 4 5
# Default-Stop:      0 1 6
# X-Interactive:     true
# Short-Description: Start/stop apache2 web server
### END INIT INFO
```

The fields are fairly self-explanatory. This script provides the apache2 service. Other scripts can name this service as a pre-requisite. This script requires that local and remote filesystems be mounted, and that the network be up, and that `syslog` and named services be available prior to starting. Likewise, these services must not be stopped after this script has shut down the apache2 service. The default runlevels where apache2 should be active are 2 through 5, and of course, 0, 1, and 6 is where it is stopped. The X-Interactive field means that the script can require user input if it is run in such a way that a terminal is available to communicate with the script. There are other fields available as well, which are documented in the `insserv` manual page.

> These headers are called **LSB** headers, since they are defined in the **Linux Standard Base** document, developed jointly by a number of Linux distributions under the organizational structure of the Linux Foundation.

While dependencies generally do not change, the administrator can modify what run levels a script is active in. This should not be done by editing the headers. Rather, `update-rc.d` should be used to modify the run levels. For example, suppose you want apache to run only in run levels 4 and 5, and not 2 or 3, the command `update-rc.d apache2 disable 2 3` will do this.

> Many scripts provide a switch in their `/etc/default` config file that defines whether the service should run at all. When you want to disable a service completely, this switch should be used in preference to disabling the script in all run levels via `update-rc.d`.

The manual page for `update-rc.d` also documents the options `start` and `stop`, as well as a means of specifying the start or stop order of a script (using the legacy method of assigning numbers to the start and stop links). However, these are deprecated and it appears they will be removed in Jessie (Debian 8).

> If you have locally developed or third-party `init` scripts that do not include the necessary headers, Debian 7 will still boot using the old method of script ordering, but will notify you of the reasons it can't migrate to a dependency-based boot sequence.

Managing SysV scripts

The `update-rc.d` utility has already been mentioned, and is one of the primary command line interfaces for managing `init` scripts. However, there are several other utilities that are essentially a frontend for `update-rc.d` that make the administrator's job a little easier. The primary ones are `bum` and `sysv-rc-conf`.

The Boot Up Manager, or `bum`, is a graphical application for managing `init` scripts. It requires a window manager to run, and provides a nice interface showing what services are running and what scripts are enabled. In advanced mode, it will also allow you to adjust individual run levels and run order.

> As mentioned for the `update-rc.d` start and stop commands, adjusting script ordering is not recommended.

There is also a utility called `sys-rc-conf`. It uses the curses library to provide a full-screen text interface. In its default mode, it will not modify script order, although special options on the command line will allow this if you really need this functionality.

Both utilities are pretty much self-explanatory. Check the services you want, uncheck those you don't, and you can set or unset check marks for different run levels on the same script.

> Frequently, you will need to execute a SysV script manually, either to check the status, or to restart a service that requires it. Although the script in `/etc/init.d` may be executed manually, the recommended method is to use the `invoke-rc.d` command, which ensures that system policy and run level constraints are satisfied.

Third-party and local scripts

Non-Debian third-party packages often do not provide SysV scripts to start and stop their software's background processes, and you may need to write your own. Even if such scripts are provided, they may need to be modified to follow the Debian standards, particularly if they use prepackaged functions available in other distributions that differ from those in Debian.

Writing `init` scripts is a whole subject in itself. However, the Debian `initscripts` package includes a `/etc/init.d/skeleton` script that can be copied and modified according to your needs. The requirements for such scripts are defined in *Chapter 9, The Operating System* of the *Debian Policy Manual* (available as a Debian package and at `http://www.debian.org/doc/debian-policy/`) and *Chapter 20, System Initialization* of the *Core Linux System Base standard* (available at `http://refspecs.linuxfoundation.org/lsb.shtml`). The latter also provides for some standard functions in `/lib/lsb/init-functions` to assist in script coding.

Network administration

Basic to any system is network access, either to allow others to use its services, or to allow users to access services on other systems. There are two main ways of setting up and controlling networking, the static `/etc/network/interfaces` file, and the more dynamic Network Manager.

The interfaces file

This is the traditional method for setting up networking on a Debian system. It involves a series of files in `/etc/network`. RPM-based systems such as RedHat Fedora and SuSE Linux use a different layout in `/etc/sysconfig/network` that is managed by their own utilities.

The `/etc/network/interfaces` file is probably the simplest way to get a network up and running. While it must be edited manually, it is easy to understand and a minimum number of configuration lines are needed to handle most situations. In fact, the Debian installation process will set up this file for you. If you use the same networking configuration as you used for installation, the network will work immediately and require minimal tweaking. In fact, a minimal interfaces file is usually sufficient for most servers that aren't part of a cluster. Even if you do use an alternate method for network configuration, such as Network Manager, the local loopback interface is usually left configured in the interfaces file to keep the alternate configuration uncluttered, since it requires only basic configuration and doesn't normally need to be modified.

The interfaces file, while it can be very simple, also offers many options for more complex setups. You can configure wired, wireless, **VLAN** (**Virtual Local Area Network**) and Bridge interfaces, IP tunnels, and **Point to Point** (**PPP**) interfaces. Each interface can be configured to use DHCP or a static IP address, with both IPv4 and IPv6 supported as well as Novell's IPX protocol. A simple interfaces file is shown as follows:

```
# This file describes the network interfaces available on your
# system and how to activate them. For more information, see
# interfaces(5).

# The loopback network interface
auto lo
iface lo inet loopback

# The primary network interface
allow-hotplug eth0
iface eth0 inet static
  address 192.168.3.52
  netmask 255.255.255.0
  gateway 192.168.3.1
```

Lines beginning with `#` are comments, of course. The purpose of other lines is as follows:

- `auto lo`: The `lo` interface is brought up whenever `ifup` is run with the `-a` option, as it is during system initialization
- `iface lo inet loopback`: This defines the basic loopback interface ; the address is always `127.0.0.1` or `::1` for IPv6
- `allow-hotplug eth0`: This brings up Ethernet 0 if it is available and plugged in
- `iface eth0 inet static`: This defines Ethernet 0 as an interface with a static IP address
- `address`, `netmask`, and `gateway`: These define Ethernet 0's address, net mask, and the default IP gateway, respectively.

Simple and to the point. This file was actually set up during Debian installation and works as is. Of course, there are many other options available which are documented in the interfaces manual page that allow you to handle much more complex configurations. The details on setting up the interfaces file may be found in the interfaces manual page. It includes information on setting up IPv6 and many other protocols.

In addition to the interfaces file, there are a number of scripts in the `/etc/network` hierarchy that are related. In particular, the subdirectories `if-pre-up.d`, `if-up.d`, `if-down.d`, and `if-post-down.d` contain scripts that are run automatically when interfaces are brought up or down. In addition, specific scripts can be identified in the interfaces file to be executed when a particular interface is brought up or down (this is especially useful in configuring Bridges). The major disadvantage to using the `/etc/network/interfaces` file is that there is no provision to configure **Virtual Private Networks** (**VPN**). However, in general, these can be configured using command line tools.

> Additional details and examples may be found in *Chapter 5, Network Setup* of the Debian Reference Manual (`http://www.debian.org/doc/manuals/debian-reference/ch05.en.html`).

Network Manager

As flexible as the `/etc/network/interfaces` configuration is, many administrators prefer a more graphical interface to network configuration that may be used in a more dynamic network environment. Network Manager is most often used to manage wireless connections. It consists of a background process that does the actual connection management and has both a command line and a graphical utility that allows you to configure and control the managed connections.

The graphical utility displays available access points and provides a menu and an easy way to configure the connection. It can also be used for wired connections and can manage VPN connections to a private network as well. The main disadvantage of Network Manager is that it does not handle bridging, VLANs, or the IPX protocol. Of course, command line tools can be used to supplement Network Manager in order to configure these options, or the interfaces file can be used to manually configure them while Network Manager handles the rest.

There are other packages that provide a GUI interface for network configuration. One of the main ones is `wicd`. Some users prefer it as it handles wireless connections in a different manner that may allow certain wireless cards to work better, but it has fewer features.

Combining methods

It is possible to combine both the interfaces file and Network Manager methods of network configuration, with each responsible for a portion of the configuration. This technique might be used when certain features are required that only one of the methods support. For example, Network Manager doesn't handle network bridging, and the interfaces file generally can't be used to configure VPN connections. If you needed both, you would set up bridging using the interfaces file and configure your VPN connection using Network Manager.

For those unfamiliar with network bridging, a good example would be a development system that runs one or more virtual machines that require direct access to the network (meaning its connection must behave as if it is an actual interface with a direct network connection). The basic setup looks like the following diagram:

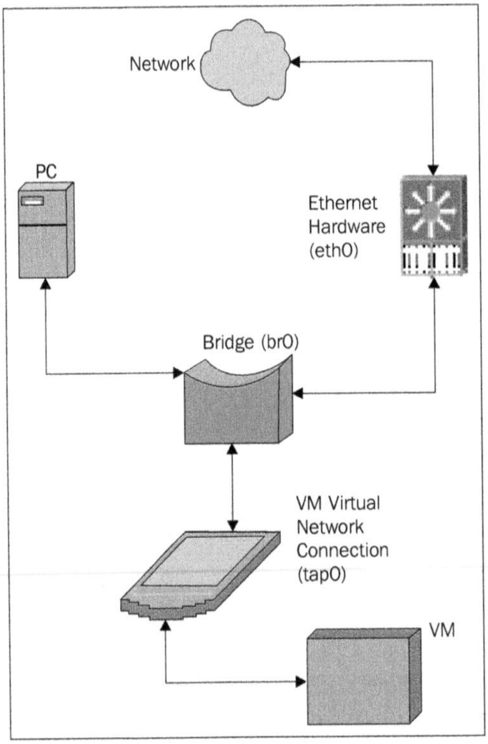

Note that the host machine now uses **br0** instead of **eth0** as its primary interface. The bridge interface uses eth0 to connect to the actual network. The **VM** (**Virtual Machine**) will set up its own network interface (or you will set it up). These are generally set up as a tap or tunnel interface (hence the name **tap0**).

To set it up, the basic interfaces file might look like the following listing (assuming the hardware Ethernet card is eth0):

```
# TAP setup
auto tap0
iface tap0 inet manual
      pre-up /usr/sbin/tunctl -t tap0

# Bridge setup
auto br0
iface br0 inet dhcp
      bridge_ports eth0 tap0
```

This sets up a TAP device using the `tunctl` command to create the device. It must appear before the bridge or it won't be there when the bridge device is initialized and attempts to connect it to the bridge. The bridge setup creates the bridge interface and uses DHCP to obtain the IP address. The `bridge_ports` line indicates that it bridges traffic to the real interface (eth0) and the tap0 interface, which will be used by the VM. I've left out the loopback entry for clarity. In this example, VPN and wireless connections are left for Network Manager to handle.

More about network bridging may be found in the `bridge-utils` package, and network tap and tunnel interfaces are covered by the `uml-utilities` package.

Which method?

Network Manager is automatically installed with the GNOME Window Manager. It is especially useful in a laptop environment. For servers, the interfaces file is probably the best and most flexible option. Of course, if you require certain features available only in one or the other, use whatever provides them, combining the two techniques if necessary.

> Don't attempt to control the same interface using both methods. While Network Manager will refuse to manage a connection defined in the interfaces file, and the `ifup` command will generate an error if it attempts to set up an interface already controlled by Network Manager, it is possible to circumvent these protections.

Filesystem maintenance

There are two types of filesystem maintenance: partition and content maintenance. The former includes periodic checking of the filesystem's underlying structure and metadata, modifying the partition layout, and low-level backups. The latter involves monitoring and controlling the space used by files as well as file backup and recovery.

Partition maintenance

Although modern journaling filesystems are quite resilient, they will, on occasion, suffer an error in the underlying infrastructure. The reasons are many and include power fluctuations, hardware failures, and certain types of kernel failures. While the last is extremely rare in Debian stable releases, it does happen, especially if third-party kernel modules that are not part of Debian are installed or if the kernel has been modified locally for some reason.

Filesystem Check (FSCK)

Maintenance involves running the **Filesystem Check program** (**FSCK**). If the system is rebooted frequently, as is the case with laptops or workstations, or the partition is unmounted and mounted frequently, this will normally happen automatically. EXT3 and EXT4 filesystems default to every 39 mounts when originally created unless otherwise requested. This may be changed using the `tune2fs` utility which can also set a time-dependent check interval instead of mount count dependent.

> Although it is possible, periodic checking should not be disabled. Journaling filesystems in general are always marked clean and so Linux will not recognize when such a system may have problems.

If your system is always up and the partition in question is never unmounted, you may want to arrange for a periodic reboot of the system, either via the `shutdown -rF` command that forces a filesystem check, or by using `tune2fs` to set a time-dependent check interval that is less than the reboot interval. Of course, if problems are found, you must have access to the physical console in order to answer the questions about how to fix them.

An alternative is to never check the filesystem except when problems are obvious or likely. Normally, after a failure that could potentially cause filesystem infrastructure errors, the system will need to be rebooted anyway, if it isn't forced. This is the time to run the FSCK manually in maintenance (single user) mode, or to force the check by having a short, time-dependent check interval set. Again, if problems arise, someone will need access to the physical console in order to answer questions.

> To speed up periodic filesystem checks, use EXT4 instead of EXT3. In most circumstances, checks are anywhere from 2 to 20 times faster for EXT4.

Partition resizing

Partition resizing may be required if you need more space. To get a quick overview of your disk space usage, use the `df` command. There is also a disk usage (`du`) command that summarizes file and directory space. Refer to the manual pages for details.

If you must resize a disk partition, the procedures are fairly straightforward but there are some considerations.

> There is always a risk in modifying your partition layout. Make sure you have current backups prior to modifying the layout.

If the partition is being expanded, there must be room to expand it. If you are using **Logical Volume Manager** (**LVM**), this can be as simple as adding a physical volume to the volume group if there is not enough space left in it. If you are not using LVM, or if you have multiple partitions configured on the same logical volume, then there must be free space available on the physical disk or logical volume following the end of the partition to be expanded. If there isn't, it must be created somehow. If the partition is to be shrunk, space is not an issue, although you may want to move or expand other partitions to use the space freed up by shrinking. Also, it is sometimes necessary to move partitions around. This is not necessary if you use LVM and assign one partition per logical volume.

Moving or shrinking a partition may only be done with unmounted (offline) partitions, since it requires moving files and risks corruption if any files are in use. Some filesystems, EXT3 and EXT4 in particular, may be expanded while the partition is still mounted, however, since this doesn't require moving any files, just modifying the filesystem metadata.

While each filesystem architecture has appropriate tools for resizing and there are simple tools for managing the partition table, the primary tool for managing partitions is `parted`. There are other, mostly commercial tools, but `parted` does pretty much everything that is necessary, is available as an easy to use graphical utility (`gparted`), and it is free. There is even a live CD version you can boot to manage your partitions regardless of what operating system is installed. Many Windows administrators use it quite successfully. It handles both enlarging and shrinking partitions as well as moving them, and will handle many different filesystem architectures, and ensures that the partition table matches the filesystem sizes.

> Unfortunately, neither `parted` nor `gparted` will not allow you to expand a mounted partition. If you must expand a partition while it is in use, you must delete and recreate the partition with the same, identical beginning position, force a reread of the partition table, and then use the appropriate filesystem resizing commands. This is extremely dangerous and should never be used for resizing the root partition.

> The procedures for modifying partition layout are straightforward. Note that if you aren't booted from a `gparted` live CD or similar utility disk, you cannot unmount partitions required to run the necessary utilities and operating system services.

To manually modify your partition layout:

1. Ensure there is adequate space for the expanded partition, or to hold the partition being moved. If necessary, shrink or move other partitions or expand the logical volume.
2. You must ensure the partition table matches the resized or moved partition exactly. Failing to do this can result in corrupted or lost data. `gparted` will handle this for you automatically.
3. To shrink a partition, it must be offline (unmounted). Resize the filesystem first, then modify the partition table to match the new size.
4. To expand a partition, modify the partition table first, then expand the filesystem. If you are doing this with a mounted partition, you must use the procedure outlined previously.
5. To move a partition, you must first create a new partition of the same size as the original. Then you must unmount the current partition, copy the data to the new partition exactly, and delete the old partition.

In all cases, the partition must be clean prior to modifying or moving it, and should be checked afterwards prior to mounting it. The `gparted` utility or similar will handle the steps above automatically, including the necessary filesystem checks, data movement, and partition table modifications.

Note that either `gparted` or the manual procedures may be used on a live system, provided the partitions being modified can be unmounted, or if a mounted partition must be modified, it is only being expanded and `gparted` is not being used.

> Unless you must expand a partition while it remains mounted and in use, the recommended procedure is to boot from a `gparted` live CD. This greatly simplifies the whole process, allows modification of all partitions, not just those that aren't required for operating system services and necessary utilities, and reduces the risk of corruption.

Backups

In general, there are two types of backups: low-level image backups, and file-level backups.

Low-level backups

Low-level disk image or so-called Bare Metal backups, are byte-level copies of a full partition or even a complete logical or physical disk. Some utilities will only include used sectors in the copy, thus reducing the size and speed of the backup and restore operations, but this is not always the case. When restoring such a backup, some sort of media, such as a live CD, is required in order to boot up the software to restore the image.

Full disk byte-level backups are useful if you need to duplicate or restore a system quickly, as long as the disk being restored is the same or larger. Partition backups of this type may also be done, but in order to restore them you will need some way to restore the partition information to the disk partition table.

Low-level backups are useful in two situations:

- When a system must be replaced and restored quickly with identical hardware
- When a system needs to be duplicated many times on identical hardware

A good example of the latter is when a company provides workers with preconfigured systems all with identical or nearly identical initial configurations. In this case, it is easy just to restore the disk from a standardized copy whenever a new system is required or an old one needs to be returned to its original condition for a new employee.

File-level backups

File-level backups can be as simple as a file-by-file copy of everything in your directory hierarchy, to a backup that takes into account the filesystem metadata structures and that doesn't store duplicate data (commonly called **data de-duplication**). Restoration generally requires a minimal installed system, or a live CD. File-level backups do not have the ability to restore boot sectors or partition tables, so these must already exist or be created prior to restoring your files. Many file-level backup utilities provide the ability to back up only files that have changed since a previous backup.

File-level backups are most useful when individual files or directories are lost or corrupted, or need to be reverted to an earlier version, as only the files necessary need to be restored. This is not possible with low-level image backups.

Backup utilities

There are many backup utilities available and they vary from simple ones appropriate for individual systems, to complex backup suites appropriate for managing backups for multiple production systems and clusters.

The simpler utilities generally provide file-level backups that are written to external media or even a remote network location. They frequently provide options for incremental backups, where only changed files are copied after the first, full backup. Mostly, these are command line utilities which can be scripted and executed periodically via a CRON job, although there are graphical front ends available. The disadvantage of most of these are that in the event you need to restore after a complete disk failure, you must have some other means of restoring the partition information correctly, and of recreating the boot sector information properly so the system will be bootable.

Among the more common of the simple utility commands are `rsync` and `tar`. Frequently, these utilities are used in the more complex backup software to actually store the data. If you use one of the EXT filesystems, the `dump` and `restore` commands are of particular interest, because they understand and take into account the filesystem's metadata and are thus faster and more efficient than the simpler copy utilities. The disadvantage, of course, is that restores may only be done to an equivalent EXT filesystem. Other utilities such as `rsync` can restore to a completely different filesystem type, although certain metadata, such as file ownership and permissions, may be lost if the type is too different, such as backing up from an EXT4 filesystem and restoring to an NTFS partition.

More complex backup software is sometimes capable of so-called Bare Metal backups. These combine small, low-level backups of (or at least the ability to recreate) the non-filesystem structures such as the partition tables and boot sectors, with file-level backups of the filesystem contents. Many are multisystem backup solutions that can be administered from a central location and which can store the backups on various media in various locations. Usually, these multisystem suites include the ability to define and control backup schedules, contents, and locations as well as provide for off-site archiving.

Choosing your solution

Which backup software you choose is somewhat a matter of taste, but there are some guidelines. For quick and dirty backups of individual files, the standard `rsync`, `tar`, and `cpio` utilities are usually sufficient. For more routine backup of individual systems, one of the software packages that provide for configuring and scheduling automatic backups, both full and incremental, is your best bet. If you have multiple systems to back up, one of the major backup suites that provide central control, scheduling, and storage is best. We will discuss this further in *Chapter 7, Advanced System Management*.

In all cases, if your backup solution doesn't automatically take care of it, be sure to include a rescue or live CD that includes the software necessary to format and partition the disk drive, restore the files, and recreate the boot information. Some backup packages, such as `Mondo`, include the creation of such bootable media as part of their software.

> Don't neglect backups. Even the most resilient VM environment with multipath **Network Addressable Storage** (**NAS**) can fail in unexpected ways that will corrupt your data. I am aware of one such environment where the UPS was disconnected in a way that removed power from both the NAS system and the VM host. Although the Debian system used a non-cached journal for its filesystem, the NAS was buffering the journal writes. When power was lost, the journal was incomplete, and the disk ended up quite corrupted. Lesson learned.

System logging

Another one of the system administrator's responsibilities is to manage the system logs. Debian systems by default log information that can tell an administrator how the system is being used, provide warnings and error messages that can indicate problems with software or hardware, and even provide early signs the system is being attacked or misused.

System logs are handled by the `rsyslog` package, and normally reside in `/var/log` and its subdirectories. Various software packages and especially those that provide important services, such as DNS, FTP, E-Mail, and HTTP (Apache), often do extensive logging that may include entries that allow activity to be tracked and warn of potential problems or misconfiguration. The package documentation includes information on how to configure what is logged and where.

The logging facility

The `rsyslog` system logging facility in Linux provides for various options, facilities, and log levels. The options control what happens when a message is logged, such as whether it is sent to the console if it can't be logged in a file, whether the **process ID (PID)** is included in the message. The facilities provide a means to divide messages into various areas according to what subsystem is involved, such as AUTH for authorization messages, CRON for scheduled jobs, KERN for kernel messages. Most software that uses the system log provides configuration items to control the options, files, and facilities it uses for its messages. In addition, and most important, are the levels of log messages, which determine how important a message is.

Log levels detail which messages, of the many that might be sent to the system log, actually get logged. This varies from the EMERG level, which only involves messages that essentially mean the system is unusable, down through ALERT (immediate action required), CRIT (critical), and ERR (errors) to WARN (warning conditions), NOTICE (normal but significant), INFO, and DEBUG. Setting the log level to any of the latter three can generate a significant number of entries and use a lot of disk space as well as requiring significant system overhead.

For that reason, there are some guidelines as to what should be logged:

- Production systems should only log EMERG, CRIT, ALERT, ERR, and WARN levels. NOTICE, INFO, and DEBUG should never be logged on a production system unless absolutely necessary.
- Development systems should log those levels mentioned in the previous point, along with NOTICE and perhaps INFO levels to provide information necessary to the software developers. DEBUG may also be used when necessary.

The idea is to provide the necessary information without unduly burdening a system. In particular, NOTICE, INFO and especially DEBUG levels can produce massive amounts of data that are generally unnecessary in a stable production system.

Log data is frequently used to analyze how the system is being used, who accesses it, what activities are being performed, as well as to notify the administrator of things that need attention.

Controlling the logs

Even production system logs will eventually grow to the point where they take up a significant amount of disk space, and this is even more of a problem with development systems that follow the preceding guidelines. One of the administrator's duties is to determine how much log data should be kept, and manage the files appropriately.

All distributions, and Debian is no exception, provide by default a job or jobs that run periodically to close the current log files, mark them with a cycle number, and open new, clean files for logging. In Debian, this is provided by the `logrotate` package. While this package is primarily concerned with log files, it can be used for any other files that grow constantly and need to be cycled. Detailed documentation is provided with the package, but the basic idea is that each log file is checked and if it is over a certain size, it is closed. Then all cycles of the log file are renamed, and if necessary, those over a certain age or cycle number are deleted. A new log file is then created to continue logging.

You can configure how many cycles are kept, or even how old the cycles can be before they are deleted. The primary choice here is how long you wish to keep log entries. The defaults installed with each package reflect the experience of many administrators and are usually appropriate in most circumstances.

Monitoring the logs

So, does an administrator need to wade through all of the log entries daily? That would be an extremely tedious task, and is really not necessary. A number of packages exist in Debian that will scan the logs for certain conditions and email the results to the administrator for further checking and action. The most common is `logcheck`, which checks the latest log cycles against a database of entries that an administrator might be interested in. It then emails the important ones to the administrator for further checking. There are also packages that perform various analysis tasks, such as email statistics or HTTP access statistics, using the system logs often combined with other information sources. They may be found using the Debian package management search facilities.

> What package you use to check the logs, or even whether you use your own scripts based on string searches, is not important. The critical thing is to check the logs regularly. They can give you timely warning of impending hardware issues, software instabilities, programming problems, and attacks on your system.

Display managers

Straight servers, as opposed to development servers, generally do not require a display manager. Of course, development servers and those servers that do provide the ability to log in to a managed display environment do require both a display manager and a window manager. The former handles the creation and security of the X-Windows display environment and resources required, while the latter handles the actual desktop environment presented to the user.

There are several major environments, each with its associated Display and Window Managers. The two major environments are GNOME and KDE. Both support a variety of graphic toolkit libraries, so that most applications that run in one will run in the other, provided the necessary services are available. These services are usually installed as a dependency when the application is installed if you don't install the basic meta package for either GNOME or KDE. So if, for example, you like the `KcacheGrind` tool for browsing program profiling data, but are using GNOME, you can go ahead and install and use it under GNOME. It will work fine. Likewise, if you prefer the **K Display Manager** (**KDM**) that comes with KDE to the **GNOME Display Manager** (**GDM**) provided by GNOME, it will work just as well.

Given this interoperability, why choose one over the other? It is mostly a matter of personal preference. As mentioned in the first chapter, KDE is usually preferred by European users, while GNOME is more of an American preference. Our main concern in this section will be where to find configuration files or applications for each.

Where did my desktop go?

Both GNOME and KDE, like the new Windows 8, have abandoned the old desktop metaphor for a more activity or task oriented look. It takes some getting used to and can be disconcerting at first. Covering the changes from the old look to the new would take a book for each Desktop Manager! However, the home sites for both KDE and GNOME provide tutorials and documentation to help you get started. If you prefer the older desktop metaphor, both GNOME and KDE provide ways to set this up as well.

GNOME

The current GNOME release in Debian 7 is 3.4. If you install the `gnome` meta package, all major GNOME applications as well as the window and display managers, will be installed. Configuration is pretty straightforward, as the user menu provides a System Settings application to access the major settings of your workspace in order to alter how it looks and feels.

Modifying the GNOME login screen, GDM3, if you don't want the default behavior, requires manual editing of `/etc/gdm3/greeter.gsettings` and `/etc/gdm3/daemon.conf` as the root user. Then execute the `dpkg-reconfigure gdm3` command.

> Part of the reason for this is that GDM is being integrated more fully into GNOME, and is being moved to the `dconf` settings framework from the old GNOME 2 `gconf` based settings. At some point, the GNOME control center should provide the appropriate utility but, at this time, there is no official GDM3 setup utility. An unofficial utility called `gdm3setup` exists, but has not found its way into Debian, yet.

KDE

The current KDE release for Debian 7 is 4.8.4. The `kde-full` meta package will provide all KDE applications as well as the window and display managers. The KDE user environment provides a System Settings application just as GNOME does, but it is a bit more comprehensive as it includes the ability to configure KDM, the display manager responsible for the login screen. In fact, because of this, some administrators use KDM as the display manager, even though the default session may be GNOME.

Other desktops

XFCE and LXDE are the most common alternatives to KDE or GNOME, although there are others. Neither one provides a display manager for login screens, although LXDE recommends LightDM, a lightweight display manager. XFCE and LXDE (as well as LightDM) retain the old desktop metaphor, and are designed to place a minimal load on the system, making them appropriate for older hardware.

> During the time *Linus Torvalds* abandoned GNOME3, he ran XFCE.

Like both GNOME and KDE, both XFCE and LXDE provide a system settings application to control the look and feel. LightDM also provides a graphical settings utility.

Showing your best face

Take time to at least look into the settings for your chosen display manager. Unless you are running a server that never sees a graphical login, this is the first and last thing your users see. You may also want to look into appropriate backgrounds for your users' desktops. They don't need to be fancy but they do make an impression.

Summary

The tasks of an administrator are many and include the responsibility for what services the system provides (especially how they are started and shut down), network configuration, system backup, filesystem space management, system operation (system logs), and providing the face the system shows to the world. We've covered some of the issues in each of these areas, although comprehensive coverage of any of the subjects could take several books. One subject not covered here that must be covered in depth is basic system security. We will cover this in the next chapter.

6

Basic System Security

One of the most critical tasks performed by system administrators is setting up and monitoring system security. Debian provides some assistance here, with special packages that help in hardening your systems, but this is only the beginning. In particular, you must pay attention to how you set up the root account, how to block improper access to your systems, and how to monitor your system for security problems.

User administration

One of the first things to consider is how to set up user groups and how to manage the root account. Although this can be changed any time, it should be done just after installation when changes will have less impact. The two basic issues are how to set up default user group assignment, and whether the root account should be disabled.

Default user group

Traditionally, there are two ways to set up the default group assigned to a new user. The first is to have everyone assigned to a single users group. This will allow all users on the system access files and directories with group read (and execute) permissions, and write to files with group write permissions.

The other way is to give each user his own groups, usually with the same name as his user ID. This is the default in Debian, and this scheme is often referred to as user private groups. If user A wants others to be able to access certain files or directories via the group permissions, someone with system privileges that allow group modification must add the appropriate user IDs to user A's group.

> At one point, a single users group was common practice. Best practice at present, though, is to use user private groups.

This is similar to the most common way to handle developer's access to each other's files. In this case, though, a new group, such as `web-dev` or whatever you feel is an appropriate group name, is created and the developers are assigned to it as necessary. A similar technique is used for some administration tasks as well. For example, an `ftpadmin` group that is allowed to modify the FTP server directories and files in ways that the normal (and especially the anonymous) ftp user cannot. Careful creation and assignment of groups can facilitate proper user access to files while preventing undesired access or modification.

User and group maintenance is handled by the standard command-line functions, such as `useradd`, `usermod`, `userdel`, `groupadd`, `groupmod`, and `groupdel`, all documented in the `passwd` package. Of course, there are GUI utilities available for user and group maintenance as well.

ACLs

While the traditional user/group/world permissions structure is adequate for many systems, there are times when more fine-grained control is required. This may be handled by using **Access Control Lists** (**ACL**). ACLs are implemented using the extended attributes available in various filesystems and are available by default in the EXT filesystems normally used in Debian Linux. The details may be found in the Debian `acl` package. In particular, check out the manual pages for the `getacl`, `setacl`, and `chacl` commands.

While ACLs are useful, there are some issues to be aware of. For example, most graphical file managers do not support them, and some utilities (EMACS comes to mind) clear the file ACL list when updating a file. This can be addressed somewhat by setting a default ACL for the directory, but non-default file ACLs will still need to be reconstructed if they are lost. Another issue is performance. On some filesystems, the existence of an ACL delays the initial file access due to the additional access verification required. Since this occurs only on the initial access, its impact is often minimal in practice. Finally, there is the issue of backups when you use ACLs. Most backup utilities now recognize ACLs. In Debian Linux, both `rsync` and `tar` now have options to allow them to recognize and back up ACLs, but they are only handled if you use the proper command options. The EXT backup utilities dump and restore also handle ACLs. However, some utilities may not recognize or handle ACLs properly, so always check the package documentation and manual pages if you use Access Control Lists.

Note that, if you do use ACLs, you are not required to use them for all files and directories. It is quite possible to set them on only those files and directories that need them. Judicious use of file ACLs and default ACLs set for certain directories will help streamline ACL management.

The root account

Root access to a system is a serious issue. Anyone who knows the root password can do great damage, and the more people who know it, the greater the chance of the password getting into the wrong hands. To avoid this problem, the `sudo` package provides the ability to run commands as if one were the root user (including, if desired, a shell with full root permissions) without requiring the root password, only the user's own password and proper authorization. The advantage of this is that authorized commands are logged with the user's ID, providing an audit of who actually performed the command.

When `sudo` is used on a system, the only remaining use for the administrator password is when the system is booted into maintenance (single user) mode. Most Linux distributions, including Debian, require the root password before providing the root shell prompt in single user mode. However, this requirement can be bypassed in several ways by someone with access to the physical console. Therefore, many administrators completely disable the root password. When this is done, booting into maintenance or single user mode no longer prompts for the root password.

By disabling the root password completely, root-level access to the system via any method other than `sudo`, other programs that provide root privileges to normal users (also known as **setuid** programs), or via boot into single user mode is not possible. Note that, since booting into maintenance mode no longer requires a password, physical access to the system console must be controlled in some other way. This may be done by physical means, by requiring a password for the system boot via **BIOS** (**Basic Input/Output System**) or **UEFI** (**Unified Extensible Firmware Interface**), or by password protecting the GRUB or other system boot loader.

> Best practice is to disable the root account login completely. **Ubuntu** now does this by default, and Debian is moving in that direction. Make sure you either restrict physical access to the console or password protect the boot process.

The /etc/sudoers file and files in the /etc/sudoers.d directory are where sudo access is configured. The details are provided in the sudo package documentation. Briefly, access to commands can be allowed or restricted by individual user, group members, or even lists and can allow access to commands depending on the remote host from which the user is accessing the system.

Debian hardening packages

Debian provides several packages to assist the administrator in securing the system. They are all meta packages, and include:

- harden: This installs harden-environment and harden-servers
- harden-clients: This prevents installation of software clients that have the potential to expose critical information or allow unauthorized access to your system
- harden-environment: This installs tools for intrusion detection
- harden-nids: This installs tools for network intrusion detection
- harden-servers: This prevents installation of services that are potentially insecure and could allow unauthorized access to your system
- harden-tools: This installs tools to help enhance and analyze system security

There are other hardening packages that install tools to analyze or audit systems remotely, and help developers create more secure programs. The packages can be found by searching the package cache for "harden". One way to do this is the command apt-cache search harden.

Installing any of these packages is just a start, and won't automatically make your system secure. They are just a way of installing groups of security related packages, or preventing certain packages from being installed if they have potential security issues. In particular, if you install harden-environment, harden-nids, and harden-tools, you will also need to consult the appropriate package documentation and configure them properly to detect and analyze security issues, issue the proper warnings, or take the necessary actions.

> One thing to be aware of is that some of these packages prevent the installation of certain services, such as an FTP server. If your server must provide FTP services (for example), then first install the appropriate hardening packages. After the install completes, install the FTP package confirming that you want to remove the hardening package. That way, you at least know that insecure services other than FTP have not been installed. To maintain that assurance, periodically test what `harden-servers` would remove if installed. This can be done, for example, by running `apt-get -dry-run install harden-servers`, and examining the output to see what would be done.

Firewall tools

One thing that the hardening packages do not provide is tools for protecting your systems via firewalls. This absence belies their importance in securing your systems, as a short search of Debian packages will show many tools for building firewalls. They vary from simple to complex, and from command line to full graphic interface. Nearly all are frontends for **IPTABLES**, the Linux kernel firewall modules and associated commands, and produce appropriate configuration files. Some provide a simple configuration language that is more readable than the standard `iptables` commands, which the tool then translates into the proper commands for you. Some provide a way of defining firewall policies, which are then translated into proper `iptables` configuration commands.

> Even if your system is already behind a firewall, it is good practice to provide its own firewall as well. This multilayer approach provides additional protection in case the first firewall is somehow compromised.

Of course, with the variety of firewall packages available, it is difficult to recommend any particular package over the others. Each has strengths and weaknesses. However, if we restrict ourselves to the more popular packages, there are a few general recommendations that can be made.

First, for desktop and development systems which don't require extremely complex configurations, **firestarter** (for GNOME) or **guarddog** (KDE) are good starting points. They are oriented towards beginners but have advanced options that can be useful to more experienced users. Both are graphical applications. A special case is **fireflier**, which actually analyzes the applications traffic on the system and recommends rules. Mason is a similar application, but it does not offer a graphical interface.

For servers or systems that require more robust protection, consider **fwbuilder**. It is similar to many enterprise firewall management systems and can provide configuration not only for Linux (both IPTABLES and IPCHAINS rules), but also BSD, Mac OS/X, and Cisco access-lists as well. Configurations for multiple servers can be kept in one place and installed remotely as needed. Refer to `http://www.fwbuilder.org/` for more information.

A popular alternative is **Shorewall**, which can also handle traffic shaping and IPsec to some extent. Shorewall uses text configuration files rather than a graphic interface. More information may be found at `http://shorewall.net/`.

In all cases, for Debian Linux, the firewall packages control traffic by generating the IPTABLES rules used by the kernel modules to recognize, analyze, and control network traffic.

IPTABLES

IPTABLES, which supersedes the old IPCHAINS code, is the generic name for what is actually a group of kernel modules and applications used to define and control Linux kernel firewalling. It actually includes modules and applications to provide IPv4, IPv6, ARP, and Ethernet Frame packet filtering as well as some stateful inspection of packets. There are many options for filtering, depending not only on the packet characteristics (such as protocol, source and destination addresses), but on how the packet is being handled, such as whether it is just entering the system, being forwarded, exiting to the network, needs address translation (such as **Network Address Translation** or **NAT**), related to an established connection. There are several good books available on IPTABLES, or you can start with the documentation on the `www.netfilter.org` website, which is the home of IPTABLES code as well as many related projects.

> There is a project, **NFTABLES**, which is slated to replace IPTABLES in the kernel. It is still under development and at the time of writing, there is no official Debian support (either in Debian 7 or the testing release for Debian 8). However, there are compatibility packages in the works, and once the code becomes part of the official Linux kernel, official Debian packages are expected to follow.

Since most firewall packages provide their own ways to define your firewalls and output the appropriate iptables configuration commands, it is not necessary to understand all of the gritty details of IPTABLES, but a good administrator will want to understand the basics for a couple of reasons. First, it will help in understanding the capabilities of the firewall configuration software, since the features will be based on what can be done with IPTABLES, and second, it will be needed if you use something such as fireflier or mason, which propose rules and expect you to modify or delete them as required for your specific environment.

Of course, beyond understanding what is possible, it is necessary to figure out what is required for your firewall.

Basic firewall design

There are many books and reams of Internet advice on building firewalls. The classic work on the subject is *Building Internet Firewalls* by *Elizabeth D. Zwicky, Simon Cooper,* and *D. Brent Chapman, O'Reilly Media*. However, for our present purposes, we'll cover some basic design principles.

Inbound opens

Any time someone can open a connection to a system, that system can be attacked via that connection. This doesn't refer to inbound traffic in general, especially since much of this will be related to connections the local system established. It refers to the request from a remote system for a new connection to a local service. This is usually called an inbound open as it involves an initial request by a remote system to open a connection on a specific IP port.

Of course, if your system is a server that provides services to remote users, you must allow requests for services your server provides. Just don't allow any other inbound requests, and if you can, limit the source address of the requests unless the service is to be provided to anyone and everyone.

> Limit inbound requests (opens) to only those absolutely required to provide particular services to remote clients. Do not allow any other inbound traffic unless it is on or related to an established connection.

Outbound traffic

In general, outbound traffic is legitimate, and many administrators do not restrict traffic originating on the local system going to remote systems. Unfortunately, there are cases where this is not advisable. A common example is when a company wishes to restrict the outside services its employees can use (such as preventing the use of YouTube because it is inappropriate for them to be using it during working hours). Another example, though, is the case where a system has been compromised and starts contacting a remote command and control system for orders and additional malicious software to install.

Both cases may be handled by at least logging, and in many cases restricting outbound traffic. In most cases it is sufficient to limit outbound opens (requests for a new connection).

> On a personal system, outbound opens need not be restricted unless company policy requires such restrictions. On a server, outbound opens should be restricted to those services that the server requires for proper operation. Outbound traffic should be allowed only if it is on or related to an established connection.

Local loopback traffic

Most administrators are not concerned with traffic on the local loopback interface. This is because such traffic is often necessary for proper operation of the local system. It is also rather difficult to analyze in order to determine what is necessary and what may be safely blocked without affecting normal operation. The major reason to firewall loopback traffic is that if rogue software is installed on the system by a virus or worm, then that software has more avenues to further attack the local system over the unprotected loopback interface. It may allow a minor compromise to exploit the opening to become a major system takeover.

The major trade-off here is whether the likelihood of compromise and the resulting potential for damage justify the additional time and effort required to analyze and create a proper firewall for the loopback interface.

> If a system is subject to frequent, serious attacks, consider firewalling the local loopback interface as well.

The perimeter network

Probably one of the most important ways to protect private networks while still providing services available to the public Internet is by using a perimeter network. Often called a **De-Militarized Zone** (**DMZ**), it is a buffer between attackers and your internal network.

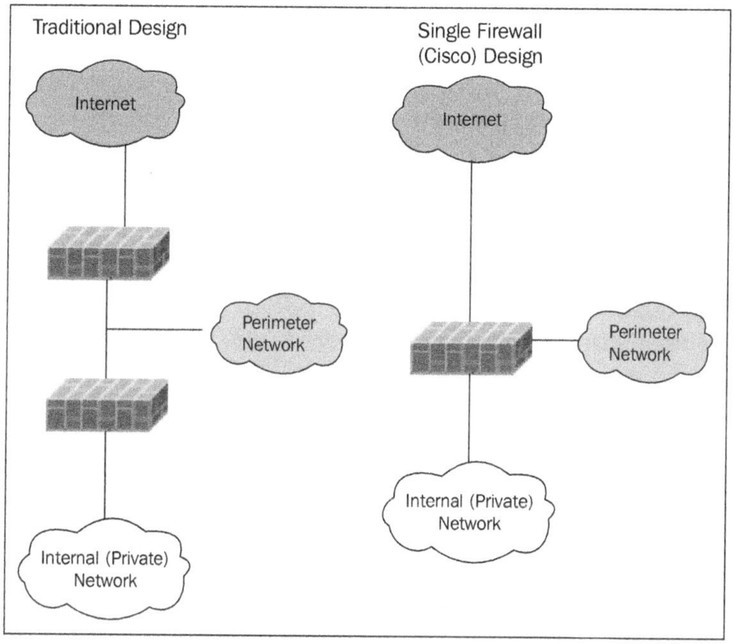

In the previous diagram, there are two architectures given. The traditional design uses two firewalls with the perimeter network placed in between them. The reason for this is that if the external firewall which is exposed directly to the Internet and attack is compromised, the attacker still has to get through the internal firewall before he has access to systems on your internal network. Experience has shown that firewall compromise is uncommon enough that a single firewall can be used reasonably safely, as shown on the right. The dual firewall architecture is still preferred for high security environments.

In all cases, the only systems that can be accessed from the Internet are those on the perimeter network. Those servers must not have any access to internal servers through the firewall. Internal servers can connect to the perimeter systems and thus allow two-way communication, but servers on the perimeter should never be able to initiate connections to internal systems. This prevents a compromised server from further endangering your internal network.

> No matter how careful you are, any server connected to the Internet will be attacked, and attacked frequently. Sooner or later, one of those attacks will succeed. No server that allows any outside access is completely immune to compromise. Best practice for any system, not just Debian, is to place Internet servers on a perimeter network in order to protect your internal systems and data in the event an Internet server is compromised.

So, now you have your system properly firewalled. As mentioned previously, you will still be attacked, and eventually compromised. The next section deals with how to detect both the attempts and any compromise as soon as possible.

Intrusion detection

Debian includes a number of intrusion detection applications. There are three basic classes: **Network Intrusion Detection Systems** (**NIDS**), File Monitors, and System Scanners. The former works by scanning network traffic to detect attempts to discover and exploit allowed network connections. The latter works by scanning a known clean system, then monitoring it for new, deleted, and modified files.

NIDS

Network Intrusion Detection basically involves monitoring network interfaces, analyzing all the packets seen, and providing alerts when certain attack characteristics are seen. On Debian, the primary tool for this is **Snort**. Snort will be installed if you install `harden-nids`, mentioned previously. Other packages are also available in Debian as well.

Snort can be paired with a package called `fwsnort` to not only detect potential attacks, but block them dynamically via adding IPTABLES rules when attacks are detected.

One caveat is that NIDS can only analyze traffic they actually see. They will see all traffic on whatever interfaces they monitor (in fact, Snort will see it before IPTABLES does, ensuring that all traffic is analyzed). However, if your system is protected by an external firewall (for example, if it's on a perimeter network), it will only see packets that are allowed through the external firewall. Because of this, NIDS may be of limited use unless it is run on the external firewall. Nevertheless, it is still useful to detect attack attempts that manage to get through the external firewall.

File Monitors

The second level of intrusion detection involves monitoring the files on the system. There are several good monitors that will alert you to new, deleted, or modified files, usually filtering the reports so they include only changes that indicate a potential compromise. The most commonly used File Monitor is **Tripwire** and that is what is installed by the `harden-environment` package. However, Tripwire is now owned by a commercial enterprise that sells proprietary versions. While open source tripwire is still available, many administrators are switching to **AIDE** (**Advanced Intrusion Detection Environment**) or **Samhain** as alternatives.

> Configure your file monitors carefully to catch important changes and filter out as many false positives as possible without filtering out the true positives.

The importance of filtering your results can't be overemphasized. An alert or report with too many false positives will frequently be skimmed at best or ignored at worst, and can result in missing a true positive indication of compromised files.

System scanners

System scanners include packages that scan for possible rootkits that may be installed or active on your system, and virus scanners. The packages `rkhunter` and `chkrootkit` are two of the most used rootkit detection packages. The `Tiger` package is a somewhat more comprehensive scanner that uses `chkrootkit` and Tripwire or AIDE as well as its own scripts to perform a full audit of your system's security. After the first audit of your clean system, `Tiger` will alert you to changes in your system's vulnerabilities.

The only major function absent from `Tiger` is virus scanning, which can be handled by the `clamav` package, which also provides live scanning of email.

> Best practice is to set up regular system security audits.

A final word on remote logging

One of the first things an accomplished hacker will do once he penetrates a system is attempt to erase all signs of system compromise. This includes removing entries from log files, hiding files, and network connections so they can't be shown using normal utilities, and so on. They may even go so far as to install their own compromised versions of your intrusion detection software, and your file and system scanners that won't report any sign of their illicit activities. One of the best countermeasures for this is to set your system up to write your system logs and NIDS and scan results to a remote system. Many scanners also provide ways to encrypt and verify configuration files and scan databases to protect them from compromise as well.

> If your system is subject to frequent attacks, set up remote logging, reporting, and alerting, and secure the configuration files and databases of your system and file scanners and your Intrusion Detection System.

Summary

System security is one of the most important duties of an administrator. Ensure that your system is protected by setting up proper policies for users and groups, and hardening your systems (especially servers) when exposed to attack from the Internet. Firewall tools are useful in blocking attacks, and intrusion detection should be used to discover any system anomalies as early as possible.

We've now been through pretty much all of the major administrative areas of Debian Linux, not counting individual software suites. Next, we will cover some advanced administration techniques.

7
Advanced System Management

In this final chapter, we'll cover briefly several advanced administration subjects. Remote backups and configuration administration will be covered, and we will briefly look at cluster management. Finally, we will look at one of the most useful administration tools for any Linux system, Webmin.

Remote backups

If you're in charge of one or more systems that are installed at a distant location, backing them up individually can be a large chore. Fortunately, there are a number of packages that can help. Most backup packages, even those intended to create a backup of a single machine, have options to send the data to a remote location for actual storage. Of course, any of the packages with this capability can be used on multiple machines. However, there are two popular packages that not only provide backup services to multiple hosts from a central location, but provide for management of backup cycles and automated runs as well. They are **Amanda** and **Bacula**. Of course, other such packages exist, and there are some excellent third-party backup solutions as well. However, both Amanda and Bacula are provided as part of Debian, so they are free as well as able to handle many systems and a variety of backup media.

Amanda

For many years, the **University of Maryland** (**UoM**) Computer Science department was the source of quality, free software that rivaled or even surpassed proprietary solutions. The **Advanced Maryland Automatic Network Disk Archiver** (**AMANDA**), is one such solution. Although no longer supported by UoM, it is now hosted on SourceForge, where it remains in active development. In addition to the free Community edition, there is a paid Enterprise edition that includes additional features, such as a graphical configuration utility.

> The Amanda site notes that some Linux distributions are far behind in the release they include. This is not the case with Debian. Version 3.3.1 is included in Debian 7 Wheezy.

Originally oriented heavily towards centralized tape backup of many networked systems, it now supports disk and even cloud-based storage of backup data as well. Amanda requires a software client running on the systems to be backed up. Clients are available for most Unix type systems, as well as Mac OS/X and various Windows releases. The server side will run on pretty much any Unix- or Linux-based system. This makes Amanda especially useful for large, heterogeneous sites.

Amanda uses standard tape and disk file formats, which allows standard tools, such as `mt` and `tar`, to be used to browse or even recover data if desired. Amanda provides for parallel backups of many systems at once, backup file management; restore utilities that are easy to use, and several layers of security (including encryption of the backup data over the network, and encryption of the backup files). Amanda is implemented as a single central server that communicates with multiple clients.

A discussion of Amanda configuration could take up a whole book and is very dependent on the type of backup media you use and the systems you are backing up. However, briefly, the community (free) version of Amanda must be configured manually, by adding subdirectories and configuration files to the `/etc/amanda/` configuration directory. Refer to the documentation that comes with Amanda, or visit the `www.amanda.org` website for further information. Also, several commercially published books on backup and recovery have chapters on Amanda configuration.

Bacula

Bacula is another popular free backup package. It is designed to be more modular than Amanda. Like Amanda, it requires a client on the system to be backed up. In addition to the client, however, there is an administrative console service, a status monitor service, a backup director which controls the actual backup operations, a storage service that keeps the actual backup data, and a database service where the backup information and catalogs are maintained. Of course, except for the client (which must reside on the systems being backed up), these services may be spread among different systems or consolidated on a single server.

Bacula configuration is object-oriented, in that you define clients, jobs, schedules jobs, file sets (to be backed up), storage pools to hold the backup data, messages (to handle emailing of reports), the catalog database, and the director which coordinates the whole thing. There are many useful functions, including some that allow restoration of a system without access to the catalog, creation of boot CDs which will allow a full, bare metal restore.

One thing to note is that the Bacula rescue CD is set up to restore disk partitions exactly as they existed at the time of the disk creation. If you need to run a bare metal restore to a system with a different disk configuration, the rescue CD also provides the fdisk utility, and you can add other utilities to it if you wish.

The Bacula director and storage components run on Linux, FreeBSD, or Solaris. It has also been reported to work on some Windows versions, Mac OS/X, and other BSD variants, although this is not officially supported. The client is available for many different systems, including various Linux, Windows, Mac, and BSD systems. Bacula is also reported to work on AIX, BSDI, and HPUX systems, although this is not officially supported.

Installing Bacula on Debian is straightforward. There are packages for each of the various parts, as well as, several meta packages. The bacula meta package installs both the `bacula-client` and `bacula-server` meta packages. The client package installs the Bacula console and file daemon (client). The server package installs the Bacula director and storage packages. There are several choices for the Bacula director, depending on what database you wish to use for your catalogs. The packages may be installed either via the meta packages or individually, as desired.

As with Amanda, Bacula is a comprehensive and complex solution. Aside from the comprehensive documentation available on the Bacula web site, `http://www.bacula.org/`, there are several books available that cover it well, including one available from `www.packtpub.com` (*Network Backup with Bacula [How-to]*, by *Yauheni V. Pankov, [PACKT] Publishing*). Briefly, though, Bacula uses text files for configuration, in directories under `/etc/bacula`. The Bacula console package provides a graphical console application, although in practice the interface is actually a command line utility.

Other backup systems

Of course, Debian offers other backup packages as well. They are less complex than Amanda or Bacula, but more suited to smaller environments. Most use standard file archiving utilities, and offer remote storage options (either via standard remote file specification or by using a client and server approach). Some offer backup cycle management utilities, backup encryption, communications encryption, and even de-duplication when using special backup storage formats. Synaptic or apt-cache can be used to search for these packages using the search term backup.

Some administrators prefer to keep it even simpler and write their own short scripts which use the basic archiving commands (such as `rsync`, `tar`, or the `EXT dump/restore` commands) to perform backups as a scheduled CRON job.

Beyond backups

Of course, backups are not the only issue with managing multiple, remote systems. In particular, managing such multiple configurations using a centralized application is often desirable.

Configuration management

One of the issues frequently faced by administrators is that of having multiple, remote systems all with similar software for the most part, but with minor differences in what is installed or running. Debian provides several packages that can help manage such an environment in a unified manner. Two of the more popular packages, both available in Debian, are FAI and Puppet. While we don't have the space to go into details, both applications are described briefly here.

Fully Automated Installation

Fully Automated Installation (**FAI**) focuses on managing Linux installations, and is developed using Debian, although it works with many different distributions, not just Debian. FAI uses a class concept for categorizing similar systems, and provides a good deal of flexibility and customization via hooks. FAI provides for unattended, automatic installation as well as tools for monitoring and updating groups of systems. FAI is frequently used for creating and maintaining clusters. More information is available at `http://fai-project.org/`.

Puppet

Probably the best known application for distributed management is Puppet, developed by Puppet Labs. Unlike FAI, only the Open Source edition is free, the Enterprise edition, which has many additional features, is not. Puppet does include support for environments other than Linux. The desired configuration is described in a custom, high-level definition language, and distributed to systems with installed clients. Unlike FAI, Puppet does not provide its own bare metal remote installation method, but does use existing methods (such as `kickstart`) to provide this function. A number of companies that make heavy use of distributed and clustered systems use Puppet to manage their environments. More information is available at `http://puppetlabs.com/`.

Other packages

There are other packages that can be used to manage a distributed environment, such as Chef and BCFG2. While simpler than Puppet or FAI, they support similar functions and have been used in some distributed and clustered environments.

The use of FAI, Puppet, and others in cluster management warrants a brief look at clustering next, and what packages in Debian support clustering.

Clusters

A cluster is a group of systems that work together in such a way that the whole functions as a single unit. Such clusters can be loosely coupled or tightly coupled. A loosely coupled environment, each system is complete in itself, and can handle all of the tasks any of the other systems can handle. The environment provides mechanisms for redundancy, load sharing, and fail-over between systems, and is often called a **High Availability** (**HA**) cluster. In a tightly coupled environment, the systems involved are highly dependent on one another, often sharing memory and disk storage, and all work on the same task together. The environment provides mechanisms for data sharing, avoiding storage conflicts, keeping the systems in synchronization, and splitting up tasks appropriately. This design is often used in super-computing environments.

> Clustering is an advanced technique that involves more than just installing and configuring software. It also involves hardware integration, and systems and network design, and implementation. Along with the URLs mentioned below, a good text on the subject is *Building Clustered Linux Systems*, by *Robert W. Lucke*, *Prentice Hall*. Here we will only touch the very basics, along with what tools Debian provides.

Let's take a brief look at each environment, and some of the tools used to create them.

High Availability clusters

Two primary functions are required to implement a high availability cluster:

1. A way to handle load balancing and individual host fail-over.
2. A way to synchronize storage so that all servers provide the same view of the data they serve.

Debian includes meta packages that bring together software from the Linux High Availability project, including `cluster-agents` and `resource-agents`, two of the higher-level meta packages. These packages install various agents that are useful in coordinating and managing load balancing and fail-over. In some cases, a master server is designated to distribute the processing load among other servers.

Data synchronization is handled by using shared storage and any of the filesystems that provide for multiple accesses and shared files, such as NFS or AFS.

High Availability clusters generally use standard software, along with software that is readily available to manage the dynamics of such environments.

Beowulf clusters

In addition to the considerations for High Availability clusters, more tightly coupled environments such as Beowulf clusters also require an infrastructure to manage and distribute computing tasks. There are several web pages devoted to creating a Beowulf cluster using Debian as well as packages that aid in creating such a cluster. One such page is `https://wiki.debian.org/StartaBeowulf`, a Debian Wiki page on Beowulf basics. The manual for FAI, mentioned previously in configuration management, also has a section on creating a Beowulf cluster. Books are available as well. Debian provides several packages that are helpful in building such a cluster, such as the OpenMPI libraries for message passing, and various utilities that run commands on multiple systems, such as those in the `kadif` package. There are even projects that have released scripts and live CDs that allow you to set up a cluster quickly (one such project is the PelicanHPC project, developed for Debian Lenny, hosted at `http://www.pelicanhpc.org/`.

This type of cluster is not something that you can set up and go. Beowulf and other tightly coupled clusters are intended for highly parallel computing, and the programs that do the actual computing must be designed specifically for such an environment. That said, some packages for specific parallel computations do exist in Debian, such as `nwchem`, which provides several applications for computational chemistry that take advantage of parallelism.

Common tools

Some common components of clusters have already been mentioned, such as the OpenMPI libraries. Aside from the meta-packages already mentioned, the *redhat-cluster* suite of tools is available in Debian, as well as many useful libraries, scheduling tools, and failover tools such as *booth*. All of these can be found using apt-cache or Synaptic by searching for "cluster".

Webmin

Many administrators will never have to administer a cluster, and many won't be responsible for a large number of systems requiring central backup solutions. However, even administering a single system using command line tools and text editors can be a chore. Even clusters sometimes require administrative tasks on individual systems. Fortunately, there is an application that can ease many administrative tasks, is easy to use, and can handle many aspects of Linux administration. It is called **Webmin**.

Up until Debian Sarge, Webmin was a part of Debian distributions. However, the Debian developer in charge of packaging it had difficulty keeping up with the frequent releases, and it was eventually dropped from Debian. However, the upstream Webmin developers maintain current packages that install cleanly. Some users have reported issues because Webmin does not always handle configuration files exactly as Debian intends, but it most certainly attempts to handle them in a compatible manner, and while some users have experienced problems with upgrades, many administrators are quite happy with Webmin.

As long as you are willing to deal with conflicts during upgrades, or restrict use of modules that have major configuration impacts, you will find Webmin quite useful.

Installing Webmin

Webmin may be installed by adding the following lines to your apt sources file:

```
deb http://download.webmin.com/download/repository sarge contrib
deb http://webmin.mirror.somersettechsolutions.co.uk/repository
  sarge contrib
```

Usually, this is added to a separate `webmin.list` file in `/etc/apt/sources.list.d`.

> The use of 'sarge' for the release name in the configuration is not a mistake. Since Webmin was dropped after the Sarge release (Debian 3.1), the developers update the repository as it is and haven't bothered changing it to keep up with the Debian code names. However, the versions available in the repository are compatible with any Debian release since 3.1.

After updating your cache file, Webmin can be installed and maintained using apt-get, aptitude, or Synaptic. Also, if you request a Webmin upgrade from within Webmin itself on a Debian system, it will use the proper Debian package to upgrade.

Using Webmin

Webmin runs in the background, and provides an HTTP or HTTPS server on localhost port 10,000. You can use any web browser to connect to `http://localhost:10000/` to access Webmin. Upon first installation, only the root user or those in a group allowed to use `sudo` to access the root account, may log in but Webmin users can be managed separately or in conjunction with local users.

Webmin provides extensive and easy to understand menus and icons for various configuration tasks. Webmin is also highly modular and extensible, and an extensive list of standard modules is included with the base package. It is not possible to cover Webmin as fully here as it deserves, but a short list of some of its capabilities includes:

- Configuration of Webmin itself (the server, users, modules, and security)
- Local system user and password management
- Filesystem management
- Bootup and service management
- CRON job management
- Software updates
- Basic filesystem backups
- Authentication and security configuration
- APACHE, DNS, SSH, and FTP (if you're using ProFTP) configuration
- User mail management
- Qmail or sendmail configuration
- Network and Firewall configuration and management
- Bandwidth monitoring
- Printer management

There are even modules that apply to clusters. Also, Webmin can search and allow access to other Webmin servers on the local network or you can define remote servers manually. This allows a central Webmin server, installed on a particular system, to be the gateway to all of the other servers in your environment, essentially providing a single point of access to manage all Webmin enabled servers.

Webmin and Debian

Webmin understands the configuration file layout of many distributions. The main problem is when a particular module does not handle certain types of configuration in the way the Debian developers prefer, which can make package upgrades somewhat difficult.

This can be handled in a couple of ways. Most modules provide a means to edit configuration files directly, so if you have read the Debian documentation you can modify the configuration appropriately to use Debian specific configuration techniques. Or, you may choose to allow Webmin to modify files as it sees fit, and handle any conflicts manually when you upgrade the software involved. Finally, you can avoid those modules involved with specific software that are more likely to cause problems.

> One such module is Apache, which doesn't use links from `sites-enabled` to `sites-available`. Rather, it configures directly in the `sites-enabled` directory. Some administrators create the configuration in Webmin, and then move and link the files. Others prefer to manually configure Apache outside of Webmin.

Webmin modules are constantly changing, and some actually recognize the Debian file layouts well, so it is not possible to give a comprehensive list of modules to avoid at this time.

> Best practice when using Webmin is to read the documentation and check the configuration files for specific software prior to using Webmin. Then, after configuring with Webmin, check the files again to determine whether changes may be required to work within the particular package's Debian configuration framework. Based upon this, you can decide whether to continue to configure using Webmin or switch back to manual configuration of that particular software.

Webmin security

Security is always a concern when remote access to a system is involved. Webmin handles this by requiring authentication and providing for detailed access restrictions that provide a layer of control beyond the firewall. Webmin users can be defined separately, or certain local users can be designated. Access to the various modules in Webmin can be restricted to certain users or groups of users, and detailed logs of Webmin actions are kept.

Usermin

In addition to Webmin, there is a server called Usermin which may be installed from the same repository as Webmin. It allows individual users to perform a number of functions more easily, such as changing their password, accessing their files, read and manage their email, and managing some aspects of their user profile. It is also modular and has the same security features as Webmin.

Summary

Several powerful and flexible central backup solutions exist that help manage backups for multiple remote servers and sites. Debian provides packages that assist in building High Availability and Beowulf style multiprocessing clusters as well. And, whether you are involved in managing clusters or not, or even a single system, Webmin can ease an administrator's tasks.

Index

Symbols

A

B

C

D

E

F

P

R

S

T

U

V

W

[PACKT] open source
community experience distilled
PUBLISHING

Thank you for buying
Debian 7: System Administration Best Practices

About Packt Publishing

Packt, pronounced 'packed', published its first book "*Mastering phpMyAdmin for Effective MySQL Management*" in April 2004 and subsequently continued to specialize in publishing highly focused books on specific technologies and solutions.

Our books and publications share the experiences of your fellow IT professionals in adapting and customizing today's systems, applications, and frameworks. Our solution based books give you the knowledge and power to customize the software and technologies you're using to get the job done. Packt books are more specific and less general than the IT books you have seen in the past. Our unique business model allows us to bring you more focused information, giving you more of what you need to know, and less of what you don't.

Packt is a modern, yet unique publishing company, which focuses on producing quality, cutting-edge books for communities of developers, administrators, and newbies alike. For more information, please visit our website: `www.packtpub.com`.

About Packt Open Source

In 2010, Packt launched two new brands, Packt Open Source and Packt Enterprise, in order to continue its focus on specialization. This book is part of the Packt Open Source brand, home to books published on software built around Open Source licences, and offering information to anybody from advanced developers to budding web designers. The Open Source brand also runs Packt's Open Source Royalty Scheme, by which Packt gives a royalty to each Open Source project about whose software a book is sold.

Writing for Packt

We welcome all inquiries from people who are interested in authoring. Book proposals should be sent to author@packtpub.com. If your book idea is still at an early stage and you would like to discuss it first before writing a formal book proposal, contact us; one of our commissioning editors will get in touch with you.

We're not just looking for published authors; if you have strong technical skills but no writing experience, our experienced editors can help you develop a writing career, or simply get some additional reward for your expertise.

Mastering Web Application Development with AngularJS

ISBN: 978-1-78216-182-0 Paperback: 372 pages

Build single-page web applications using the power of AngularJS

1. Make the most out of AngularJS by understanding the AngularJS philosophy and applying it to real life development tasks
2. Effectively structure, write, test, and finally deploy your application
3. Add security and optimization features to your AngularJS applications
4. Harness the full power of AngularJS by creating your own directives

---

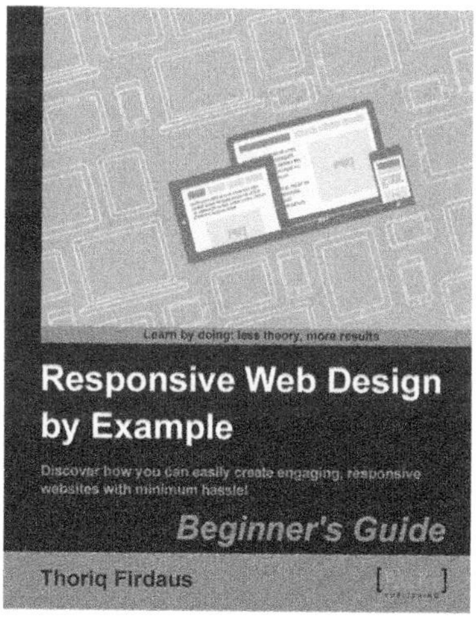

Responsive Web Design by Example

ISBN: 978-1-84969-542-8 Paperback: 338 pages

Discover how you can easily create engaging, responsive websites with minimum hassle!

1. Rapidly develop and prototype responsive websites by utilizing powerful open source frameworks
2. Focus less on the theory and more on results, with clear step-by-step instructions, previews, and examples to help you along the way
3. Learn how you can utilize three of the most powerful responsive frameworks available today: Bootstrap, Skeleton, and Zurb Foundation

Please check **www.PacktPub.com** for information on our titles

Lightning Source UK Ltd.
Milton Keynes UK
UKOW05f0651100316

269926UK00003B/70/P